Iaac *bits*

Black Ecologies

Edited by

Manuel Gausa
Areti Markopoulou
Jordi Vivaldi

With this issue, IaaC BITS is starting a new editorial phase that is intended to be more effective, ambitious and intentional both in terms of content and in the layout and configuration of the publication.

These monographic issues – presented with an experimental and proactive foundation and associated to technological and creative innovation – aim at to combining inter-disciplinary and multi-scalar exchanges with a new environmental and socio-cultural sensitivity.

This commitment to advanced culture and knowledge is well-suited to a time of challenges and changes: it conforms the conceptual framework that supports dissemination projects tied to IaaC's own production, but also to a whole network of exchanges and complicities that frame it and feed into it.

The different formats that constitute the new IaaC BITS respond to criteria of documentary coherence and expository clarity:

INTRO, main introductory inputs that help to frame each topic;
PAPERS, a set of content dedicated to background articles and theoretical contributions, argued culturally, scientifically and bibliographically;
DIALOGUES/INTERVIEWS exchanges between different approaches and research trajectories;
RESEARCH PROJECTS, a sample of projects, experimental proposals and applicative essays.

Each issue is meant to be conceived as an articulated system of voices and cross-cutting experiences focused on a central theme, which is understood as a subject for debate and proactive discussion.

Front page figure: In:Sand_Additive Manufacturing: project of IaaC, developed at Master in Advanced Architecture 01 in 2014/2015. Researchers: Anusha Arunkumar, Kunaljit Singh Chadha, Yessica Gabriela Mendez Sierra; Faculty: Areti Markopoulou, Alexandre Dubor, Carlos Bausá Martínez.

Following page figure: Homogeneous Flux – Refugee Displacement: project of IaaC, developed at Master in Advanced Architecture 02 in 2015/2016. Researchers: Philip Serif; Faculty: Jordi Pagès and Lluís Viu.

Black Ecologies

In this ninth issue (first of this new period) the term "black ecologies", as it is used in these pages, is a reference to the expression "dark ecologies" – coined by Timothy Morton in 2007.[1] It translates a new interest aimed at exploring a "new nature", not only related to architectural space but in the framework of the environment as a whole, not necessarily from the standpoint of the generalized vision of the "ecological".

While the adjective "dark" encompasses the "murky" condition of urban, peri-urban – and increasingly para-natural – scenarios and materials, its sustainable complement ("ecologies") posits the need to foster an investigation of "environmental conditions" that leave behind the Bucolic, the Platonic and/or Apollonian ideal: "environmental conditions" in which parameters of "noise", pollution, attrition, corruption and/or hybridization are considered as a substantive part of the processes being addressed.

Dark Ecologies, Black Ecologies, Dirty Ecologies and even Grey Ecologies are terms than can conjure new creative Natufices,[2] similar to what is expressed by the term "Bold Ecology" as it is defined in the *Metapolis Dictionary of Advanced Architecture*:[3]

"Instead of old nostalgic or pseudo-bucolic ecology (which freezes landscapes, territories and environments), we suggest a bold ecology (...); based no longer upon a timid, merely defensive – resistant – non-intervention or conservation, but rather upon a non-imposed, projective and qualifying – re-stimulating – intervention in synergy with the environment and, also, with technology. Not only possible, but (re)developmental as well.
An ecology in which sustainability is interaction.
In which natural is also artificial.
In which landscape is topography (and topology).
In which energy is information and technology is vehiculation.
In which development is recycling and evolution is genetic.
In which environment is field.
In which to conserve implies, always, to intervene."

A definition built around various approaches, stimuli and research scenarios and, also, around IaaC's own experimental proposals (projects and prototypes, through laboratory experiments) tinged with an operational intent, implied in a variety of contexts (economic, social, material...), which is ultimately "rough", open to being worn, used, modified, adapted but also predisposed to material and formal mutations and evolution in, from and through reality itself. The black-dark purity of the still embryonic (or uncontaminated) gives way, then, to the black-dirty warmth of those reactive and operative answers, definitively stained with materiality.

E.D. Editorial Direction

1. Morton, Timothy. *Dark Ecology: For a Logic of Future Coexistence*. New York: Columbia University Press, 2007.
2. Arroyo, Eduardo. "Natufice". In *The Metapolis Dictionary of Advanced Architecture*, edited by Gausa, Guallart, Muller, Soriano, Porras, Morales. Barcelona: Actar, 2003.
3. See the term "Ecology, active (or bold)" in *The Metapolis Dictionary of Advanced Architecture*, edited by Gausa, Guallart, Muller, Soriano, Porras, Morales. Barcelona: Actar, 2003.

Index

From Dirty Realism to Dirty Ecologies

Manuel Gausa

At the end of the 1980s, the magazine *Quaderns d'Arquitectura i Urbanisme* published an issue titled "New Narration" (Reality and Project),[1] with clearly critical intentions. Faced with the lyrical eclecticism of postmodern urban figuration, the publication reengaged with the expression "dirty realism", coined by Bill Buford in *Granta* magazine (1983). It was originally used to refer to an important literary trend – particularly in the United States – which expressed the concerns of authors like Raymond Carver, Frederick Barthelme, Tobias Wolff and Jayne Anne Philips, who were interested in a new type of direct and ordinary scenarios, portraying dry, hard and "scratchy" everyday situations[2] through a new, naked, bare, bluntly lucid and explicit narrative.

The term "dirty" described a "realism" that was no longer just content with contextual naturalism, procedural habits and relativistic weighting (or simply pragmatic "common sense") but was read in a less complacent way, depicting scenarios of conflictive and complex mutation.[3] It revealed a broken city, at the limit of this situation – and its own definition – that was neither the conventionally standard domestic suburbs nor the most institutional developmental downtowns, but rather a new type of more open and irregular peri-urbanity. The cliché of that *periphéreia* was intended as an alternative landscape but also as a "latent project": a disturbing context – in its indefinite condition – contrasted with an ideal, referential and/or symbolic center.

This definition was also picked up in Europe, in various urban investigations taking place at the time, positing a space of more ambiguous and dissolute profiles, in opposition to the post-modern eclectic and practical realism (compositional convention, ideological relativism, evocative recreation, etc.).

Previous page:
The Breath [0.7]: project of IaaC, developed at Master in Advanced Architecture 01 in 2013/2014. Researchers: Chung Kai Hsieh, Luis León López, Maria Laura Cerda; Faculty: Areti Markopoulou, Alexandre Dubor, Moritz Begle.

Der Himmel über Berlin, Win Wenders, 1987.

The so-called dirty realism was not that of prosaic and contingent pragmatism but that of a new, sharp, more precise and resistant gaze (sometimes incisively minimalist), emmeshed with the "uncertain" condition of the new, changing environments.[4]

It is interesting to note the proximity of the publication of the *Quaderns* issue (at the end of the 1980s) to the Rio Summit preparations and celebration at the beginning of the 1990s (1992), in addition to the significant influence of the involvement in a reality that was not only irregular and heterogeneous in its materializations but fragile and vulnerable in its own conditions,[5] resulting thereafter in the emergence of a global awareness that was more attuned to environmental preservation (climate change, ecological footprint, single-cycle processes, green agendas, urban resilience, rational economy and management of resources, etc.).

In a short time, this awareness of sustainability became a necessity, adopted in the urban approach in a generalized way: the paradigm of a more ecological vision offered a new protocol, often not exempted from bucolic rituals, green coloring, corrective technologies, and a new prophylactic connection with nature, which evolved into a recreated, if not revisited, landscape.

At the turn of the century, the irruption of the digital age and of a new informational and substantively interactive logic, contributed decisively to strengthening that attentive perspective towards the environment, through the reactive, responsible and responsive optimization of processes: in other words, through a greater relational engagement/connectivity within the medium, with the medium, and between different media. The periphery as an alternative landscape also gave way to the parapheria as a "multi-relational" environment.[6]

In the 1990s, this increase in a progressively interactive and "informational" exchange enhanced the exploration of hybrid combinations between programs, topologies and typologies (Land-Links, Land-Arch, Lands-in-Land, etc.[7]) and today, in the 21st century, between metabolisms and bioactive organisms. Due to technological and scientific progress, micro-organisms inserted in matter, conjugated bacteria and building energy, nano-technology applied to buildings, and evolutionary spatial crops have come to constitute some of the current fields of research.

In this progressive logic of intersection, exchange and cutting, architecture is increasingly formulated as a living and ambivalently "naturartificial" device, in a situation that amplifies the *natufices*[8] of the 1990s and expands them towards a new type of foreign metabolism, which is not only hybrid, but definitively mutated.

The new specimens thus generated do not belong to the imaginary of an agreed ecological outcome, but to a new type of non-homologated "bold ecology",[9] with strange, disturbing, turbid, dark, and often crude and unforeseen shades; in it, bio-matter processes can be generated beyond convention. The expression "dark ecologies" – coined by Timothy Morton in 2007[10] – referred to this emerging interest in exploring a "new nature", not only related to architectural space but within the framework of the environment itself, further removed from the generalized vision of the "ecological".

The adjective "dark" translates this condition of an increasingly "para-natural" nature that is "murkier" and "more perverse" ("disturbing", but also "tainted"). The term "black ecologies" as it is used in these pages forces that uneasy and disturbing quality of hard-context scenarios (those of the periphery) that were so wicked, compared to the approved "centrality".

But, it also brings them closer to the investigation of conditions (both fertile and conflictive) that are far removed from the bucolic, Platonic and/or Apollonian ideals: "environmental conditions" where parameters of contextual "noise", pollution, attrition, corruption and/or hybridization are considered to be a substantive part of the processes themselves.

These should become the center of research focused on potentially innovative models and materials, through which the "new dreams of old realities" would be built.[11]

Timothy Morton himself (paraphrasing Arie Altena[12]) emphasized this proximity to the "black series" of films and research novels, in which objectivity and subjectivity, analysis and narration, are simultaneously interwoven in a lucid, as well as implied, manner.

They approach the ecological issue not only from a natural point of view, but also from a relational one, as an interdependent system of open, non-predetermined, unprejudiced relations.[13]

"Dark ecology puts hesitation, uncertainty, irony, and thoughtfulness back into ecological thinking.

The form of dark ecology is that of noir film.

The noir narrator begins investigating a supposedly external situation, from a supposedly neutral point of view, only to discover that she or he is implicated in it.

The point of view of the narrator herself becomes stained with desire.

There is no metaposition from which we can make ecological pronouncements. Ironically, this applies in particular to the sunny, affirmative rhetoric of environmental ideology. A more honest ecological art would linger in the shadowy world of irony and difference. The ecological thought includes negativity and irony, ugliness and horror."

The current influence of Bruno Latour (P*olitics of Nature, 2000 / An Inquiry into Modes of Existence*, 2001) is evident in that unprejudiced view of new emerging processes: actants and/or inter-actants. It is interesting to compare the proactive and provocative force of Latour's vocationally holistic (and interactive) perspective with the most distanced and fragmented vision proffered by Derrida in the 1980s, and its intellectual and cultural influence on the investigations of the broken and unstructured city[14] being carried out at the time.

Then, stark, dry, hard, "dirty" minimalism – and *c(l)inical de-constructivism* – were the responses to a decidedly "non-harmonic" reality. The use of the word "dirty" could be also be applied today to a new eco-systemic thinking. The "dirty ecologies" built around experiences at IaaC (and its involvement in new experiments under way today) reflect many of the considerations exposed above; nevertheless, they are also tinted with a productive and operative agenda of involvement in a reality (economic, social, material, etc.) that is definitively "rough". They are not intended to be laboratory experiments (endogenous prototyping) but rather "pilot experiences" (exogenous prototypes open to use, modification, adaptation, etc. but also to mutation and evolution, materially and formally). Rather than *hyper-objects*[15] one might talk of *proto-environments*, decisively called on to operate (and, therefore, to get dirty) somewhere in between.

It is curious to observe how the new "dirty ecologies", contrasted with the minimalist and stark responses of "dirty realism" (the quasi-abstract debugging of a loss-making reality), translate the dynamic, prolix, effusive, often exuberant (quasi-baroque) drive of a new logic (digital and material at the same time), called on to celebrate a new proactive and productive reality; perhaps because the former evidenced the definitive death of a dream (the "American Dream") and the latter revealed the emergence of a new vital energy (that of the fertile cultivation of a new informational age). That new energy is capable of generating more efficient (optimized and techno-environmentally "mediated") novel experiences – and new spatialities – between habitat and habitats, mean and means; standing up to convention through a critical-productive reading that would refer to the one generated between "reality" and "realities", from three decades ago, and nevertheless projecting it towards less skeptical and more promiscuously generative new dimensions.

We5: project of IaaC, developed at Master in Advanced Architecture 01 in 2013/2014. Researchers: Alessio Verdolino, Hriday Siddharth , Alejandro Martínez del Campo, Tobias Grumstrup Lund, Ricardo Perez; Faculty: Javier Peña, Rodrigo Rubio, Oriol Carrasco, Stefanos Levidis.

Following double page: Industrial background of a surface mine storage place, with mining minerals and brown coal in Poland. **Photo: Mariusz Prusaczyk on Unsplash.**

References :

1. Mateo, Josep Lluis, "Reality and Project", in *Quaderns d'Arquitectura i Urbanisme*, nr. 177 *New Realities* (1988), pp. 12-17.
The "new objectivity" advocated by Quaderns would compared the "metropolitanism" of the modern city to the urban lyric of the traditional city. The issues 17 (Rigor), 1987, 176 (Voces cruzadas), 177 (Deslizamientos) 178 (Nueva Narración), 181- 182 (Geografías) and 183 (Sobre la ciudad) would be paradigmatic of that moment.
See also Mateo, Josep Lluis. "No existe el centro", in *Quaderns d'Arquitectura i Urbanisme,* nr. 175 (1987).

2. "Dirty Realism is the fiction of a new generation of American authors. They write about the belly-side of contemporary life - a deserted husband, an unwed mother, a car thief, a pickpocket, a drug addict - but they write about it with a disturbing detachment, at times verging on comedy.
Understated, ironic, sometimes savage, but insistently compassionate, these stories constitute a new voice in fiction." Appointment of Bill Buford. See Buford, Bill. "Editorial". In *Granta Magazine*, nr. 8 (1983).

3. "Dirty realism" (realismo sucio) is the name by which the English-speaking critic has ended up baptizing the new literary style imposed on its country by the last generation of North American writers. The new style (...) owes a large part of its success to its capacity to bury its deepest roots into the heart of a society undergone, for many years now, by the disillusionment of consumerism and by the despair that the death of the great American dream provoked. The novels of young and dirty realists are bare and stark stories, spectral and mechanical landscapes inhabited by lonely people without a past or a future: their life is reduced only to survive in the best possible way in a society that condemns them to isolation and anonymity beforehand, in a world from which all idealism has already been banished").
See Llamazares, Julio. "Dirty Realism". In *El País* (1987, May 20).

4. Mateo, Josep Lluis. "Reposiciones hacia el fin de siglo". In *Quaderns d'Arquitectura i Urbanisme,* nr. 164-165 (1985), p. 38. See also Meili, Marcel. "Periferia. Una carta desde Zürich". In *Quaderns d'Arquitectura i Urbanisme,* nr. 177 (1988); Solà-Morales, Ignasi. *Territorios.* Barcelona: Gustavo Gili, 2003.

5. Brundtland, Gro Harlem. *Nuestro futuro común.* Madrid: Alianza (1992), p. 765; Meadows D., Meadows D.L., Randers J. *Más allá de los límites del crecimiento.* Madrid: El País Aguilar (1992), p. 355; Romero, José Juan. "Los límites del crecimiento después de Río 92: ¿más allá del "desarrollo sostenible"? In *Revista de Fomento Social*, nr. 48 (1993), pp. 11–40.

6. The old urban notion of "periphery" (peri-pheros, the city displaced around it) seems to give way to a new concept, the "para-feria" (para-pheros, the city displaced by the margin ... and on its margins) in which the city would pass from being a single place to a "place of places", really and virtually diverse, irregular, differential and (potentially and qualitatively) (re)orientable and/or interlaceable.

7. See the concept "Land Links" in Brayer M. A. and Migayrou F. *Archilab 01.* Orleáns, 1999; as well as in various texts appeared in the issues 217 (Land-Arch), 219 (Topografías operativas) y 224 (Destellos) of *Quaderns d'Arquitectura i Urbanisme.*

8. The expressive term Natuficios is due to Eduardo Arroyo (Nomad Archs). See Gausa M., Guallart V., Muller W. "Natuficios". In *The Metapolis Dictionary of Advanced Architecture.* Barcelona: Actar, 2001.

9. See the term "Bold Ecology" in *The Metapolis Dictionary of Advanced Architecture*, edited by Gausa, Guallart, Muller, Soriano, Porras, Morales. Barcelona: Actar, 2003.

10. See Morton, Timothy. *Dark Ecology: For a Logic of Future Coexistence.* New York: Columbia University Press, 2007. See also Morton, Timothy. *Ecology Without Nature: Rethinking Environmental Aesthetics.* Cambridge: Harvard University Press, 2007 and Morton, Timothy. *The Ecological Thought.* Cambridge: Harvard University Press, 2010.

11. In reference to "What dreams are made of": *"We are such stuff as dreams are made on, and our little life is rounded with a sleep"* (William Shakespeare in "The Tempest") collected in the final phrase of the film noir "The Maltese Falcon" (John Huston, 1941): *"it's of the stuff that dreams are made of".*

12. See the reflections of Arie Altena: https://ariealt.net/2014/10/06/dark-ecology-attempt-at-a-reading-list/.

13. See Morton, Timothy appointed by Arie Altena.

14. From Latour work see Latour, Bruno. *Politics of Nature: How to Bring the Sciences into Democracy.* Cambridge: Harvard University Press, 2004; Latour, Bruno. *An Inquiry Into Modes of Existence.* Cambridge: Harvard University Press, 2013.
From Derrida see Derrida, Jacques. *La diseminación.* Madrid: Fundamentos, 1997; Derrida, Jacques. *La voz y el fenómeno.* Valencia: Pre-textos, 1985 and Derrida, Jacques. *La escritura y la diferencia.* Barcelona: Anthropos, 1989.

15. In reference to the hyper-objects proposed by Latour and other authors.

Ecologies and Ecosophies: A conversation

Areti Markopoulou and François Roche

In recent years, a growing number of architects have taken an interest in the writing and thinking of theorists like Timothy Morton, Bruno Latour, Slavoj Žižek and others loosely associated with what we define as Black Ecologies.
In January 2018, François Roche and Areti Markopoulou took part in an online conversation to speculate on how their work is related to this approach and how it can be productive for architecture in its present and future. The following transcript of that interchange has been edited for clarity.

François Roche In relation to the debate between naturalism and artifice brought up by black ecologies, I feel part of the 18th century, when Vaucanson's automata generated a serious polemic between vitalism and machinism.
In the pursuit of the Plato-Aristotle dispute about the notion of mimesis, which corrupts the ideal city for the first time or which could be used as an intercessor to the human nature and its environment, I cannot ignore Oscar Wilde's aphorism from "The Decay of Lying": "For what is Nature? Nature is no great mother who has born us. She is our creation. It is in our brain that she quickens to life. Things are because we see them, and what we see, and how we see it, depends on the arts that have influenced us." So, in this sense, the debate is not new, even if we pretend to ignore these "déjà vu", "déjà entendu". One of our contemporary problems, because of the technological endlessness flight forward, is how debates are permanently being developed looking on the proto-relation between naturalism and artifice dictated by philosophical symmetry. But in contrast, Deleuze and Negri described the tangling of this initial dualism: "A more profound response to these arguments requires that we recognize the mistake in posing an ontological division and even opposition between human life and machines... Our intellectual and corporeal developments

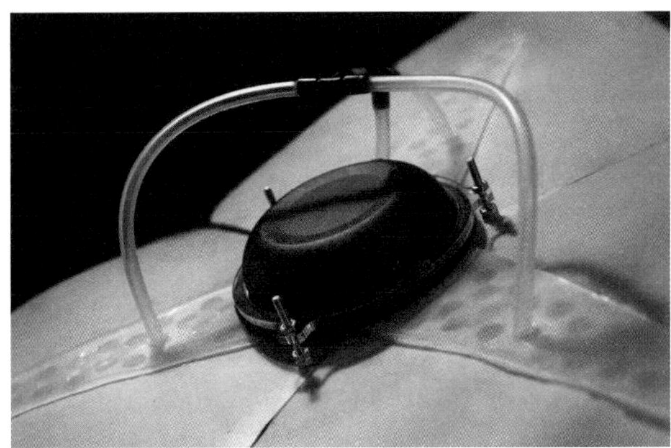

Previous page:
R&Sie(n), "I'mlostinParis" Paris - France, 2009. Structural development and construction of the green prototype. Courtesy of François Roche.

Soft Robotics Prototype B - SoRo_Lightweight Passive Shading System: project of IaaC, developed at Master in Advanced Architecture 01 in 2016/2017. Researchers: Nasser Ghannam, Guoliang Zhang, Mohamad Al Chawa, Dongliang Ye; Faculty: Areti Markopoulou, Alexandre Dubor, Angelos Chronis.

are inseparable from the creation of machines internal and external to our minds and bodies. Machines constitute and are constituted by human reality".
In this sense, we cannot ignore the co-dependencies, the correlation between nature and artifice, between human machines and its creation, from the Golem to the AI.
It's nothing else but the mirror of ourselves.
The discourse about technological singularity, mainly about artificial super intelligence, that will abruptly trigger runaway technological growth resulting in unfathomable changes to human civilization is a hoax: this Robocalypse is pure nonsense... We are the machines! It's important to spot, to scout the procedure of paranoia as the main gasoline and subjective power of our post-capitalist era. We have to face the role of media propaganda in all this issue, eschatology as a part of a global merchandising, the manipulation of fear as the main toxic junk bond.

New-Territories with Michigan-Ann Arbor/ M4, Concrete[i] land, Makkasan - Bangkok, 2015. Robotic production from recycling matter where human psyche and rejections meet in their states of chemical transformation. Courtesy of François Roche.

Areti Markopoulou Although the debate between naturalism and artifice per se is not new, our relationship with artifice in today's context of hyperconnecting bits and atoms is undoubtedly revealing unprecedented questions about our "self", other "selves" and its/their position in a hybrid world.
I cannot help observing and participating in this accelerated society, both eager and powered with ever-growing tools, to discover mental, emotional and physical wilderness. What we know, feel and see is never enough. Millennials, immersed in virtual and mixed-reality worlds, cyborgs with augmented capacities and senses, or countries granting passports to AI humanoids... All this showcases a society running at much higher "bits-per-second" speeds than the philosophical debates on the dualistic separation (or not) and the "ecosophic" equilibrium (or not) between nature and artifice. The empowered actions of such an accelerated society in the Anthropocene – or Capitalocene – era are the ones that position us a step away from the "déjà vu" and definitely far away, still, from any "entendu".
I always find it fascinating to enter the process of realizing the bi-directional effects and interdependencies of nature and artifice. On the one hand, we are part of a reality of natural manipulation through technological agents, which in particular is starting to mutate human nature. Global organizations, scientists or other individuals all over the globe are focused on understanding (even mapping) how nature is affected by technology. Obviously, this might be measurable or predictable, using numbers, indicators, statistics and algorithms, but what about the question focusing on the other part of the equation? We shouldn't avoid looking at how technology is affected by nature as well. Artificial intelligence means trying to bring what is, in essence, coming from life and nature, into technological products or into artifice. The performance of Artificial Intelligence and responsive technologies, for instance, is ruled by norms of evolution, mutation and adaptability, paying no attention to aesthetics. Aren't those the main characteristics of any natural or living organism, that is to say, related to Mother

Nature's DNA? In this sense, as architects and space performance creators, we trigger social interactions; therefore, we also need to thoroughly investigate how technology is influenced by nature rather than just how nature is influenced by technology. We also need to deeply experiment with such evolving technologies, looking into the hybrid or "trans-species" principles that the latter can bring to space, buildings and us, humans. And fortunately to do this, the traditional knowledge of our discipline is not enough.

FR Actually, we are forcing the scenario with symbiosis, with mutualism. If you look at the development of our last work, it's a temptation to articulate a kind of synesthesia between meanings and species that are normally distinguished separately. Mixing, tangling, intertwining object and subject, animal and human, nature and artifice, false and true, mad and rigorous, to touch the forbidden, something that normally does not fit into our traditional territories of knowledge, discipline and strategy of divisions.
I'm a product of Foucault-Lyotard, meaning involved in the Postmodern Post-Structuralist philosophy of 20 years ago, which questioned, among other things, the barriers between disciplines, intending to blur the niches of expertise, of pretending knowledge, to disassemble the fortresses that are permanently reconstructed: architecture appealing to architects, art to artists, science to scientists, professional talking exclusively to professional... All these niches of expertise determine a kind of isolation, a restricted area from where the "master speeches" perform cynically. As architects, we need to constantly corrupt this zone, mainly Beaux Arts', of emission in the expertise of the replica, in the stuttering of history, in the control of any "miasma" that may accidentally leak out. As architects, we need to define and locate the crack between disciplines, between those territories of power and discourses. Restarting from that, we could diffuse and infuse, through a workerism strategy, a de-alienation of situations, technologies, anthropotechnologies, to reveal the contradictions between different territories of desires, conflicts, affections. I was impressed by that, since my visit to *Immateriaux*, the last main exhibition at the Pompidou Center before it became a by-product. I still have the catalogue in plastic wrap, as a product of the future which never happened... So, the point is to take the risk of defining a counter egotic zone that is not directly driven by the greed of expertise, and first to escape from the white Caucasian heterosexual and Western architect gender, a pleonasm of DNA arrogance. That is why I created an avatar, as a political trans-androgyny, in 1993.

R&Sie(n) / Le Laboratoire / 2010, *Une architecture des Humeurs.* Animist, vitalist and machinist, the architecture of "humeurs" rearticulates the need to confront the unknown in a contradictory manner by means of computational and mathematical assessments. Courtesy of François Roche.

AM I am fond of the definition of the architect as a mediator, instead of a solitary creator. The architect's value lies in the capacity of fitting complex social, economic, cultural, political elements together and converting them into something solid, many times even material. I also like the fact that the Wachowskis trans women's "matrix" needs an architect to operate it, because the "matrix" is a systemic evolutionary set of complex operations creating "mixed" worlds.

This is very similar to the systemic mode of today's digital and physical merge. What we see or what we measure does not always reflect the real essence of things. And what we see is who we are, what our cultural background is. In a highly digitized and mixed world, "who I am" refers to multiple contexts. My "self" in social media could be something other than "me", since my news could be fake and everywhere. I like the use of the word "architecture" in systems as well, because architecture, etymologically, comes from the Greek words ἀρχι, which means "chief" and τέκτων, which means "builder". Any complex system requires building tectonic principles, whether in a hierarchical or in a more distributed way; that tectonics, in the age of experience and participation, transcends physical materialities and can only be "built" by deriving hybrid knowledge from different disciplines and perspectives. Your MMYST project is not only about bringing species together in a symbiotic system. It observes, predicts and eventually designs systems' performances.
One of our last works at the Digital Matter Studio has been designing building systems out of biodegradable materials. To design such systems, it's not enough just to define a form. We are also predicting and eventually designing the building's biodegradation, its inhabitation and co-existence with other organisms, and eventually its "collapse". Designing with fluxes, or designing to face collapse and death, hasn't been common in traditional architecture or planning. We have been foreseeing buildings to survive forever, for a very long time, while working only with a series of approximate data. In our work we in bring biologists or ecologists, and together we identify, create and program new systems and their metabolism. We merge living organisms with mechanical agents that are trained and acquire intelligence, with the goal of creating spaces designed to live and die. Is this dark or black ecology? Is it a mutated nature or the design and building evolution of the Anthropocene?

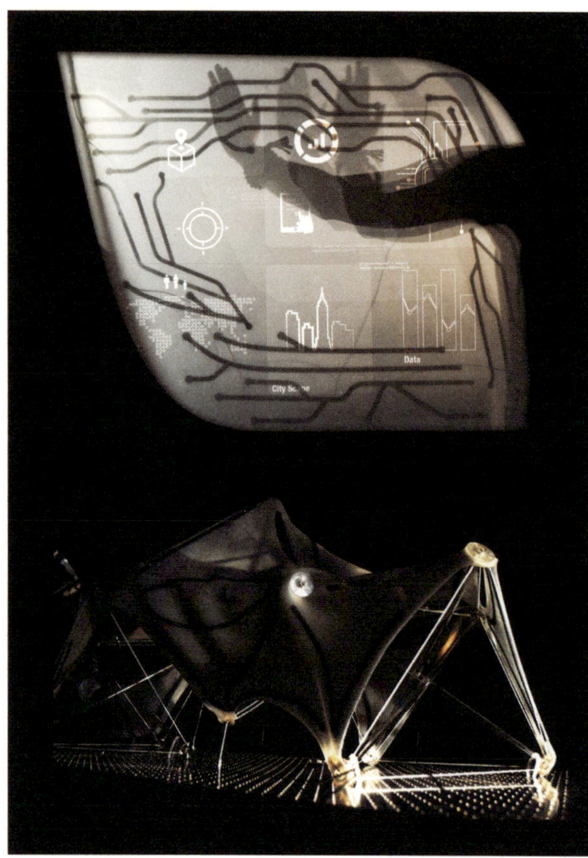

Programmable Capacitive Skin - Proskin [Graphene Architecture]: project of IaaC, developed at Master in Advanced Architecture 01 in 2015/2016. Researchers: Ingried Ramirez,Robert Staples,Burak Paksoy, Chenthur Raaghav Naagendran; Faculty: Areti Markopoulou, Alexandre Dubor, Angelos Chronis.

Tensile structure responding to user interaction - Proskin [Graphene Architecture]: project of IaaC, developed at Master in Advanced Architecture 01 in 2015/2016. Researchers: Ingried Ramirez,Robert Staples,Burak Paksoy,Chenthur Raaghav Naagendran; Faculty: Areti Markopoulou, Alexandre Dubor, Angelos Chronis.

FR When I heard about the Anthropocene as a notion related to black ecologies, I was interested in the sense of "tending our garden", following Voltaire, as a metaphor for "making" against too many metalanguages, against "Newspeak". But the garden is deeply polluted: black ecology is already intended as the recognition of the disaster. I remember the notion of tragic in Nietzsche or Walter Benjamin who spoke about the cynicism of the human condition, by nature, and the possible antidote pills for the "imagination of despair". We should recognize that we are swimming in Goya's *Pinturas Negras* and renegotiate a social-natural-artificial contract from this failure, where architecture is not used to wash, blind, ignore, falsify, jigger. We cannot deny that human beings are now responsible for the future of the planet. That is a fact we more or less share internationally. But we cannot ignore that our system of capitalist/post-capitalist values is in contradiction with the announcement effect of good intentions to save or free Willy. Photovoltaic panels produced in China with coal energy to save the roof of Paris is a hoax; Bitcoin cryptocurrency, which produces 20 megatons of CO_2 per year, around 1 million transatlantic flights; batteries for Mister Tesla made from lithium or cobalt: do you think they are the fruits of the Garden of Delights, picked to make marmalade? So, we are facing a politically correct ecology, which articulates a storytelling able to quiet our fear. And our discipline, architecture, is first intended to make and perform this propaganda to sleep our conscientiousness in a servitude mode: zero carbon at Masdar, but zero citizens too! We should question education trapped in its ivory tower of social class discrimination; I quit GSAPP because of that. We should distrust news and information published by editorials, but also reported through French, Russian, US representatives. We should question global lobotomization with IQs crashing down and social media as a new addiction and dependencies; sciences trapped in a new positivism, offering the perfect world for ideal human, transhuman, posthuman, where subhuman will be excluded by other humans. We have to face a new obscurantism coming directly and intentionally from sciences and GAFA (Google, Amazon, Facebook, Apple). The catastrophe has already happened, but we aren't panicking. We are quiet because architecture schools are still providing a zone of amnesia, in a post-Beaux Art "enchantment" for the wealthy offspring of Eastern families. Some of our European main schools are perfectly scheduled to provide the red pill (from *Matrix*)... Sorry, I have to deeply apologize for having taken the blue one, to show you "how deep the rabbit hole goes". We could accept the gift of Baudelaire based on his late obscenity to produce the right to offend, to trespass, to clash the icons (iconoclasm), to transgress the habitudes, in order to face the main discourse of Newspeak. This is really complex, and especially in architecture, where everything is already prepared to develop ignorance and amnesia. Within the supposed professional transmission of knowledge, we have to re-create a strategy of resistance: the letter R in the alphabet book by Deleuze, as in the *LOG 25* book we did with Antonio Negri in 2012, that is titled *"Resilience-Resistance"*.

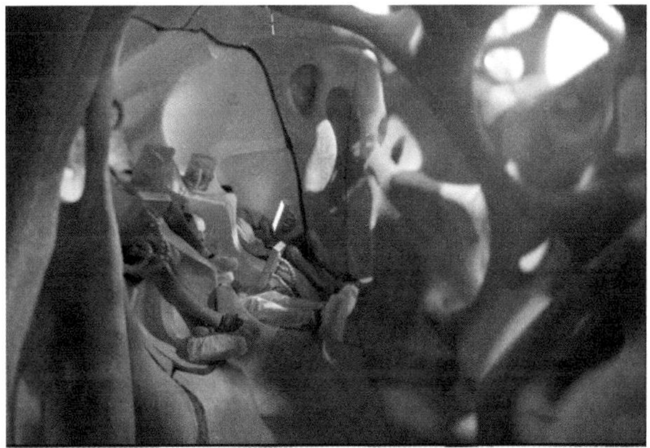

Coffee Orange Peel Bioplastic. Piel Vivo/Bio-Plastica_Material Explorations: project of IaaC, developed at Master in Advanced Architecture 01 in 2015/2016. Researchers: Noor El-Gewely, Lili Tayefi, Christopher Wong; Faculty: Areti Markopoulou, Alexandre Dubor, Angelos Chronis.

New-Territories, Hypnosis Chamber Mam, Modern Art Museum, Paris, 2005. Experiment of individual hypnosis sessions in the research and exhibition "I've heard about". Courtesy of François Roche.

AM Recognizing that our contemporary garden is polluted, principally means recognizing an ever-growing society that is highly investing in the contemporary noble lies of Plato – although those concepts are not produced with altruistic motivation, but mainly driven by the religion of capital. The first thing our architecture discipline should do, would be to expand its geological and geopolitical descriptions. The relation between nature and artifice or the relation between nature and "anthropos" are redefined in the major discourse of ecological transformations and ecological crisis: however, these discussions cannot be limited to an environmental description of measurable values like climate change and fossil fuels, without expanding to the political-economical organization of our societies throughout history. I can't help thinking about the interconnections among the discovery of fire, intellectual growth, mythology, limited liability companies, and the Agricultural and Industrial Revolutions, which Yuval Noah

Final prototype of Hydromembrane: project of IaaC, developed at Master in Advanced Architecture 01 in 2014/2015. Student: Luisa Roth; Faculty: Areti Markopoulou, Alexandre Dubor, Carlos Bausa Martinez.

Final prototype of Hydroceramic: project of IaaC, developed at Master of Advanced Architecture 01 in 2013-2014. Researchers: Akanksha Rathee, Elena Mitrofanova, Pongtida Santayanon; Faculty: Areti Markopoulou, Alexandre Dubor, Moritz Belge.

FR As we said, we are intellectually, physically, physiologically inseparable from machines; Artaud in the BwO (Body without Organs) was emitting that our desirable machinery, through temperament, fluidity, cortisol, dopamine, serotonin, adrenaline,... is Harari highlights in such an exceptional way in his book, *Sapiens: A Brief History of Human kind*.
Or Donna Haraway's "kins" and ethics of "response-ability" in an effort to define our future survival that includes the practice of justice, the emergence of multi-species assemblages and the principles of sustainability. Architecture, as design and performance, has both the responsibility and capacity to break the "Cheap Natures" – principles of labor, food, energy and raw materials that Jason Moore defines in the book *Capitalism in the Web of Life*. This requires a radical repositioning of architecture: responding to the effects of climate change but even closer to the contemporary economical-political structures. When you are talking about obscurantism, I can't help thinking that in the era of information democratization, the idea of restricted knowledge is a huge contradiction. The Obscure Men of today are the ones distorting knowledge, not the ones restricting it. It's not as direct as choosing one of the colored pills available on the shelf: we need to peel the pills, break them into their particles, define their complex logic and create new hybrid or customized ones. The goal of education is precisely teaching where to search for the tools in order to perform the breakdown and the "reform" at the same time. I work in the field of education with the certainty that I cannot teach someone what I know; that would never be enough. What we can teach is HOW to learn, how the tools to learn can be found and how distortions can be detected; how to recognize our kin and peers to learn from each other and interact to grow intellectually. Our current era of bits and atoms, which is the era of digital information and making, is simultaneously bringing new educational formats. Low-cost or no-cost e-learning, open-source culture and distributed educational programs are now accessible all over the Internet, the Fab Labs or Maker spaces. We've been running a Fab Lab at IaaC, in Barcelona, since 2007, and the access to fast prototyping, DIY technology and multidisciplinary peers radically influenced the way we think and make architecture. Visionary design for positive change, combined with fast prototyping and testing, creates a fantastic feedback loop that expands ideas and brings them to reality. In the Advanced Architecture Lab, for example, we are currently working on: the creation of energy from the roots of plants, merging electronics with growth and soil; a family of swarm robots that can adapt to weather conditions, and build with material found on site; DIY wearables and AR devices as alternative navigation systems to reorganize mobility; a flying species for urbanized coastlines that learns to collect and digest micro plastics from its environment for future use. Sometimes it is not clear if humans create machines as something separate from them, or if machines have to be integrated with humans to define novel, mixed spaces and species.

comparable with a topological fold: a torus, which co-relates inside and outside, spleen and language, pathos and overpowers, beast and human with his catatonia performances, in a kind of monism, an inseparable condition of the whole and the part, linked by fluids and subjectivities, mathematics and glitches. We are today also immersed in this ontological debate we referenced above: the ontological contradiction that the future has already been and we are in a suspended time machine, which bugs, stops and hesitates between the stuttering of what has been done and the refusal of what we don't know. Like the replica vs. the discovery, shift paradigms in contradiction, as explained by Thomas Kuhn, in *The Structure of Scientific Revolutions.*
I want to come back to the notion of ecosophy, developed by Guattari. I try to resume his concept divided into three parts: the first, ecology, is mainly referring to the human contract. Which is the unicity of a human being socialized in the swarm, in synchronicity with the multiple. The second part of the ecosophy is the current relation to nature as it is now, referring to the situation in real time, not what it should be or should have been. And the third is subjectivity: human subjectivity, including dreams, nightmares, pathologies, sociopathy, etc. – all elements which are constituent of the psycho relation with our environment and biotopes. As contemporary architects, we ignore two of Guattari's three ecologies: we often ignore the state of the social contract and never include the degree of human subjectivities. We rarely use fictions to knot and unknot realities and de-alienate managerial top-down storytelling. So, we could assume that the *tabula rasa*, not only in geography, but in the mind machine, in psychocartography, is still dedicated and oriented by modernistic values we never really denounced.
The forbidden is forbidden.

François Roche & Philippe Parreno, Hybrid Muscle Chang Mai - Thailand, 2003, Scenario: "The Game". Construction of a work and exhibition space that would generate its own electricity and thus be "unplugged" from the power grid.
Courtesy of François Roche.

AM At the moment, we transcend accepted facts in science and we accept anomalies, allowing human subjectivity to enter by default. The "paradigm shift in contradiction" of Kuhn mainly emerges from humanizing the core of science, but let's also recall Hegel's self-consciousness where subjects are also objects to other subjects, and to be one you must be many at a time.
I find it important to understand whether humans are impacting nature as one-to -one or if they are integrating it as one to many. In my idea, I perceive that we are in a moment in which we have an augmented nature that shares certain similarities with Timothy Morton's dark ecology. There is no doubt that ecology is augmented through technological agents, but it is also augmented by different "selves" with their own subjectivity, operating context and cultural stigma.
This brings a paradigm shift for architects and designers: we are not discussing the pure artificiality of our products anymore. We are designing hybrid "organisms", "new ecologies" that are evolving together with the principles of nature, instead. Affected by and affecting nature at the same time. An architecture that purifies air, heats passively, digests waste, produces food and biodegrades, triggers a radically different

Drone actuator - Translated Geometries: project of IaaC, developed at Master of Advanced Architecture 01 in 2013-2014. Researchers: Ece Tankal, Efilena Baseta, Ramin Shambayati; Faculty: Areti Markopoulou, Alexandre Dubor, Moritz Belge.

FR I would also add that we cannot use the grid of antagonism between pessimistic-idealistic, dystopia-utopia attitudes. It's too predictable and the symmetry of negative-positive is becoming a lazy game for advertising, publicity, political and goods commerce. Plugged into a post-Promethean age, experimental architecture has shifted toward a new corpus of instrumentations made out of tools like computation and mechanization, but also and simultaneously of fictions and, as we said, lines of subjectivity of our symptoms, in the trash of the Zeitgeist of "here and now". This to discover a post-digital, post-activist, post-democratic, post-feminist zone, as the somnambulist girly club in the 18th century. In this period, it was called animal magnetism, using hypnosis to create the condition of a new social contract on another exoplanet, in real time; a queer, androgynous, carnal, disturbing, disenchanted, pornographic, transient, transactional world, where scenarios, mechanisms, misunderstandings, psychological and physiological fragments are what makes up walls and ceilings, cellars and attics, schizoid

natural response than a consuming, contaminating architecture with a long-term footprint. All in all, the essence of our design and thinking is not limited to robots or mere technology: merging technological, natural and human agents, we are opening new possibilities for inhabiting architecture and space.
In those novel inhabitation models, space evolves with and through nature, not against it. We are not focusing on merely protecting our built environment from the natural environment, nor are we distinguishing the two. We envision architecture as a new living organism in synchronization with multi-species inhabitants and the environment itself, adapting to nature and evolving with it, co-existing with bacteria, animals, humans and augmented humans.
To quote Haraway: "To be a one at all you must be a many, and that's not a metaphor." The ecological wisdom of architecture cannot be a metaphor.

and paranoid; this between the lines of operative and critical fictions, triggering confusion and gut reactions, suspecting hostilities, fantasizing idealization, and even premeditating oblivion. We must use paradoxical postures and aesthetical mechanisms to highlight bio-political challenges, potentials and disorders of contemporary technologies. For this reason, we cannot forget to suspect them, from their early stages to their merchandising, not to be so harmless, not so inoffensive and innocent, beyond conventional discourses and self-conscious aesthetics.

FR For me, schizophrenia and anthroposophy are contemporary tools, like algorithms and apparatuses. We have to reconquer a lost paradise, to quote Milton, with the condition that it will never be used as an eschatologist dream, or in the Fedorov trans-human boring phantasm of eternal life, millenarist eden park, secular post-religious eternity (RealLive 2016).
In the last two years I did ACADIA and at the same time the Biennale of Chicago. In the Biennale there were mainly leftist architects focused on the idea of saving the world; unfortunately the same people were participating in the evacuation of the community center to exclude the noisy and smelly homeless from downtown – mainly back people who stayed days around the building waiting their turn to take a shower and get food.

AM We shouldn't believe in the symmetry of negative-positive, nor in any boundaries, when we deal with nature. Black ecology forces us to ask ourselves to what extent nature is bounded or not by artifice. What we know is that nature survives and develops without any need for maintenance and independent of any sort of aesthetics. In contrast, artifice decays and it requires maintenance. We need to start thinking of a new artifice, mixed with natural elements, while allowing bottom-up processes to reveal unexpected ecologies that can offer solutions to current and future challenges.
This expanded state of nature and artifice integrates both the augmented state of human culture and non-human natural systems; it operates in a complex contemporary ecosophy that can be found in a lot of contemporary work, although sometimes, indeed, it is considered more as a proof of concepts rather than as a real work. That's also something that we need, as architects, to take one step further. How can we transform our work, which is usually presented as experimental prototypes or as concept proofs, to something that can really be applied, not only to materiality but to the emotional, political sense and mentality of our society?
A change of mentality related to what a building and an inhabitant is, what the lifespan of a space is, what its materiality is and how it performs, is crucial for the ecosophic challenge. This is the moment in which, as architects, we need to take a big step forward, and that's why we need to strongly address the economical-political structures of our society, and the capitalist ecological violence. Otherwise, we will stay on the margin talking among ourselves, in a small circle, about what architecture could occasionally do, but without doing it.

R&Sie(n), Olzweg, Paris - France, 2006. Design of a Museum for Experimental Architecture. Courtesy of François Roche.

I've tried to protect, check on the internet, but all lefties wearing Prada, or Grima... looked at me and Camille, my partner, with condescendence.
Selection and discrimination in keeping with "good taste", according to Bourdieu, is the second exclusion process, after social classes.
At the opposite end, the week after, ACADIA was a meeting for geeks in short pants and jackets, playing ball or Frisbee in the courtyard, ignoring anything outside of the last Tech Fair. It's useless to tell them that the planet is burning: despite their brilliance, they will look at you with condescendence, but with a Tag Autodesk and Bentley, on their T-shirts involved in the next generation of addictive formula.
Education in architecture cannot be resumed by niches; it has to embrace complexity. I'm really surprised by the propagation of "blind mute deaf tempietto" – post AA school everywhere.
Making prototypes, small scales, with or without technologies, doesn't abolish the risk to be in this world. Architecture, within a fragment, cannot reduce complexity to the promotion of its fabrication.
The work *MythomaniaS* shown during an IaaC lecture given in Bangkok five years ago, is along these lines: small, but architecture.

SMP-joint of Translated Geometries: project of IaaC, developed at Master of Advanced Architecture 01 in 2013-2014. Researchers: Ece Tankal, Efilena Baseta, Ramin Shambayati; Faculty: Areti Markopoulou, Alexandre Dubor, Moritz Belge.

FR We ignore the dimension but, more, the limit of iconoclasm. Could we recognize, identify the contemporary Barthesian mythologies? Architects, by nature, are always surfing on the equilibrium, between synchronicities and desynchronizing, in real time and in differed times. The revolutionaries Boulee, Ledoux, Lequeux perfectly played the game of these

AM What we are urged to do is to leave the sterilized classroom environment, like the example you were giving about the Biennale. We cannot pretend that deleting the context can allow us to promote new ideas. This is impossible: a closed world, a sealed sphere, even if it is a hyper-tech biosphere, is still sealed.
If we want to promote new ideas, we need to do it in a very clear context and taking into consideration every agent that inhabits it, whether it is human or non-human. This sterilized attitude of trying to delete everything that is creating noise is not valid anymore. The key for architecture is to imagine new processes of action and performance, considering that they are required to enter our way of making; the goal for us architects is not only thinking and acting as designers, but also trying to see ourselves more as collaborators, allowing other disciplines and agents to come into this process. In this sense, black ecology doesn't refer to a starchitect who is creating high-end final aesthetics and forms anymore. It is really a kind of attitude of mediating processes that make things happen and facilitating other agents to find their place in the way of making.
It's crucial to start designing in a different way: dealing with fluxes, predicting collapses, paying attention to continuous flows of information, geopolitical realities, bio-political challenges and subjective perceptions, and integrating them all. A simply creative or iconic design which produces no change has been far from giving any solution to real challenges for too long.

DIALOGUE

ambivalences, working for the king, while preparing protests; like G. Semper in Germany, making the palace of the monarchy and ETH education temple, and at the same time designing the barricade of Dresden, the citizens proto revolt which engaged the Commune of Paris later, and its music of the swarm, to quote Rimbaud. So, first, we need to call a cat a cat:
Who are the corporate architects, who voluntary make lobotomizing design to muddy the waters?
They are the ones who are constructing a lot of ashamed and vulgar buildings.
What we are talking about is destabilizing the icons, the system organized to maintain positions of privilege, actors of the ancien régime of post-capitalism.
What an irony! We need compliant architects to produce the new hygienist temples of Gucci, LVMH, le Louvre, Vuitton and GAFA and, hopefully, there are some ready: many flattering contenders in Ithaca waiting for Ulysses to release them from their amnesic cupidity.
We are in a very accurate period-paradigm, as we were saying, wherein everything has to be re-shaped, redefined. Architecture and architects in the post-digital age are proletarians. It's the chance, in fact, to move and question education. We need to touch what is a theoretical technology, what is a disruptive technology, what is an erratic technology, etc. We need to corrupt our vision of technology, in particular its positivism and its determinism. Black ecologies need to incorporate "hope" from Pandora's box, but in correlation, in codependency, as a pursuit of our own pathologies and psychodisorders; we cannot ignore or erase human contradictions, trespassing and weaknesses.
We have to renegotiate a degree of absurdism, in the sense of Albert Camus or Lewis Carroll, including the possibility of being augmented, enhanced or reduced: by absorbing, digesting, shitting, metabolizing or mechanizing nature. In this sense, technology should be a good friend, an extension of our own escape and drama, a synesthesia to perceive complexities and contradictions, ambivalence and empathy...

15th of January 2018, New Territories Studio - IaaC
The transcription of this Conversation has been done by the Editorial Team keeping the original style of the speech.

New-Territories / M4 / RMIT, Emet - Symmetric pathologies, 2015, Screenings: Frac Orléans 2017, Chicago Biennial 2015, Venice Biennale 2013, Chicago Biennial 2015, TARS Gallery Bkk 2015. Psychotic machines, psychotic apparatuses and fragment. Bodies in verse, bodies-becoming are meeting in the stories of their symptoms. Courtesy of François Roche.

AM We need to see what comes next in technology, which is the so-called age of "calm technology" as described by Mark Weiser. Calm technology, which is a key to the Black Ecologies principles, recedes into the background of our lives, and it is not just a catalyst but the foundation for social interaction. We also need to understand that open-source culture, artificial intelligence, virtual and augmented reality, blockchain, robots, smart- and bio-materials, are not just purely technological products: they are becoming a completely new way of defining what buildings, cities and citizens are. In this era of rapid innovation, design emerges, once again, as the constructive synthesis of thought and action. Additionally, it should be open to include an architecture of systemic correlation among humans, technology and nature, inter-species collaboration, de-growth, climate justice, and new forms of social and political inclusion.

Another ecology: natural metropolitan connections

Vicente Guallart

Could the natural networks that have been destroyed by cities' urbanization be connected with the surrounding infrastructures? After decades of building infrastructures for mobility, logistics and flat land urbanization near rivers, we need to give back to nature part of what urbanization has destroyed. In order for an urban space to be natural, the networks that nature needs to house have to be designed and technologically structured.

As a metropolitan project, one of the fundamental strategies to be developed in Barcelona has to do with the connection of the Collserola Park, currently a green island, with the surrounding natural systems – especially with the coastal range to the north and the Garraf to the south. To that effect, there is a proposal that could make real the possibility of creating natural bridges to allow pedestrians, bicycles or horses to circulate through those natural spaces. This would also allow the fauna to move across the different mountain systems.

The right to travel on foot and the right to a slow pace. On the other hand, Collserola is also part of an urban system: it is a natural park in the middle of a city and it currently receives more than two million visitors each year.

Therefore, as opposed to supposing that visitors will organize themselves, proper infrastructures need to be created to organize, promote or limit, accordingly, the activities and the mobility in the park. In fact, what we know as a forest today was a very important agricultural space 100 years ago. Collserola, like nearly all of the territory, was a space dedicated to the production of food, wood and energy for the city.

Previous page:
AmpLeaf: project of IaaC, developed at Master in Advanced Architecture 01 in 2013/2014. Researchers: Kateryna Rogynska, Ramin Shambayati, Robert Douglas McKaye, Sahil Sharma; Faculty: Javier Peña, Rodrigo Rubio, Oriol Carrasco.

Collserola was planted with large expanses of grape vines that were killed off by phylloxera, which destroyed most of the wine grapes in Europe. The territory was structured and managed on the basis of large estates grouped around a number of traditional farmhouses that still exist today. Valldaura, located in the municipality of Cerdanyola, is one of them, founded by the Cistercian religious order in 1150.

Nature and Self-sufficiency

The IaaC set up a research center ingrained with the self-sufficient habitat on that estate, with the aim of learning about how nature works by coexisting with it. Nature is naturally self-sufficient. It is made up of a series of living elements that take their resources from the environment in which they are established. It can function as a part of a connected whole, as part of an ecosystem. That is what cities should be like.

Up until the 20th century, Man has always interacted with nature through the extraction of resources – while preserving nature at the same time, however, so that those resources were recurrent.

The challenge, today, lies in proposing systems and solutions using the technologies at our disposal that allow the conservation and management of nature and that will be useful in our current context.

> Cities need to be designed as systems made up of closed cycles for the exchange of energy and information. The outline of the Valldaura project we intend to develop is summed up in the idea of "learning from nature through experience".

Whereas university education, from the Middle Ages up to the present, has always been based on advanced training in a specific discipline (medicine, engineering, architecture, law, etc.), times of world structural change are moments when new disciplines should be invented. They often arise from the hybridization of a number of existing disciplines. One example is biotechnology, the fusion between biology and computation.

We propose taking on multi-scalar education: centered on human beings and their ability to interact with their immediate surroundings. The objectives would include the local production of resources (food, energy and goods) and the ability to interact globally and share knowledge through information networks.

We need to educate human beings as people in their capacity to produce the resources they need to live locally and to globally share the knowledge they accumulate: people, surroundings, planet.

Valldaura will be a multi-disciplinary environment. In 2009, we invited Meg Lowman to Valldaura to hold a workshop; she is the inventor of Canopy Biology, a discipline that studies life in the forests' upper habitat zone, which, in most cases, implies the need for lightweight structures or aerostats to provide access. With Lowman, we undertook a number of studies on forests and their biodiversity.

Valldaura will also be the location for the implementation of the first Energrid network, where different energy production sources and energy consumers will be managed using an intelligent network. Energy will be produced there using wind power systems, photovoltaic systems, biogas, biomass and hydroelectric systems.

There is an interesting phenomenon associated with energy because we know what it is, but we don't know how to measure it. Everyone knows the length of a meter, the weight of a kilo, how fast 10 km/h is, how many kilobytes are there in an image, but not how much heat a kilocalorie produces or how to produce a kilowatt.

Culturally, we don't internalize a unit of energy the same way we do with other systems. In order to interact with energy, to produce and consume it responsibly, we should be familiar with what it is. And its measurements. One of the projects that should be developed in Collserola in coming years is the creation of one or more biomass power plants. Each year, the biomass in a forest increases by 4%.

If it is not managed by thinning some trees so that the others will grow better, or clearing out the underbrush, it ends up burning or, when it snows, a large number of trees fall, which brings movement in the park to a standstill.

Nature evolves through abrupt changes like fires, which are a natural mechanism that allow the trees' seeds to spread, for example. Even if fires could be prevented, people need to increase their management of forestland to promote biodiversity.

Rural activities related with herding, agricultural uses, or the need for energy sources to heat old farmhouses, meant that the wood from fallen trees was collected as a way of obtaining naturally created resources. But, as many of these activities began to disappear, there was no longer a functional or economic reason to clear the woods and roads, or to pick up fallen trees.

That is why the creation of one biomass plant in Barcelona at the foot of Collserola, and another on the Vallès side, would create a new reason for clearing biomass from the park.

In fact, the woods are a source of knowledge that the industrialization process has led us to forget. The self-sufficient city should use the resources at its disposal and limit its impact on those places that have the most ecological value – without giving up on the management of nature and our immediate surroundings, as has always been the case.

Horses as interfaces in relation to the world

The integration with nature also has to do with other questions that connect us with ancestral processes and systems. The world changed when Man learned to tame horses and used them as a means of transportation, being able to travel at greater speeds. Horses and their abilities meant that the Arab armies could travel faster, and that the heavy Visigoth armies could invade the Iberian Peninsula in the 8th century and maintain it for centuries. Horses were our transportation system until the first train was invented and, later, the automobile. This animal, now associated with the upper classes, could be a key element in the preservation of the territory, instead.

In the crisis of 1993, I dedicated part of my professional efforts to create a company that designed graphic interfaces for multimedia systems. In 1995, we won the Mobius Award for the best graphic interface for an architecture CD-ROM at the most important international festival, held in Cannes. In 1997, we were finalists with a product for the metropolitan area of Barcelona, competing against a company owned by Bill Gates that had created an interactive application based on the Codex Leicester by Leonardo da Vinci, with a budget that was 100 times larger than ours. Fifteen years later, in 2008, we decided to learn to ride horseback, with expert endurance riders, which is similar to marathon running and has its global headquarters in Vic. A new way of learning about the natural world. Horseback riding reconnects people to the earth: you can feel it tremble when you gallop across it.

In the 1960s in Spain, only the most well-to-do classes played tennis. In the wake of the Santana phenomenon, it became a global phenomenon and a large number of tennis courts were put up in residential developments that were being built at the time.

In the 1980s and 90s, golf, which was also an elite sport, began to become more popular due to the success of Ballesteros and Olazábal.

That was the logic behind the creation of landscapes in a number of urban developments built during those years. In many cases, golf had a harmful effect on the territory, because it is one of the activities that consumes the most land for the least social use.

In the first decade of the 21st century, there has been a boom in equestrian sports in countries like France and Germany and in the Persian Gulf as a national sport.

Cantharellus Melanoxeros. Formulation of a Wooden Spatial Hypothesis: project of IaaC, developed at Master in Advanced Ecological Buildings in 2018/2019. Researchers: Pilar Aguirre, Pablo Carroto, Elisabet Fabrega & Qiao Liang; Faculty: Eduardo Chamorro Martin.

Bio-photovoltaic Panel that produces energy from bacteria: project of IaaC, developed at Master in Advanced Architecture 01 in 2013/2014 and installed at IaaC Valldaura Self Sufficient labs, Collserola Park, Barcelona. Researchers: Apostolos Marios Mouzakopoulos, Pablo Marcet, Ashwini Mani, Akanksha Kargwal; Faculty: Claudia Pasquero, Marco Poletto and Carmelo Zappulla.

And is hasn't just been horses used in rings for dressage, jumping or racing. Horses are used to travel across the land, and this has been organized into a sport in the form of endurance races.

In 2007, I met José Manuel Soto, an Andalusian singer who decided to organize the "Dakar of the horse world". It was the longest race in the world, and it was initially called "Al-Andalus".

Each year, the race covers 500 kilometers over a period of eight days. Each year, Soto seeks out 500 kilometers of rural roads in Andalusia for the competitions. We invited him to a conference called "Good News in Urban Design" ["Buenas Noticias en torno al Urbanismo"] organized by the IaaC, because we felt that highlighting the value of the territory by simply racing across it was a great territorial strategy.

On the limit between Catalonia and Valencia, I followed the traces of the Roman Via Augusta, which is marked in the Valencian territory. The road was travelled, among others, by King Jaume I during his conquest of Valencia. At present, there are plans to urbanize that beautiful place and build a real estate complex.

Near El Puig, where important operating bases were set up, the Via Augusta is a regional road, outfitted with a series of roundabouts that dot its length.

Travelling with Soto, I understood that the hope for any rural road lies in not being turned into a highway. Growth and urbanization do not always represent progress. On the contrary, in parallel to the network of high-speed trains that cross the territory, we should build a low-speed network of paths for pedestrians, cyclists and horseback riders – a network that should have the same normative value and degree of preservation as railways or national highways. People have the right to travel the planet on foot.

In a territory of networked self-sufficient cities, the right to walk or travel, using low-speed systems, and without having to make excuses to the "king-car", will be one of the fundamental arguments for the organization of the non-urban territory between cities.

In 2009, I was invited to Princeton University by the dean of the architecture school, Stan Allen. There I ran into Mario Gandelsonas, co-founder of Oppositions, the historical magazine published in New York. Mario told me that he was completing a study on transportation infrastructures for the 21st century.

- "Trains?" I asked.

- "No. That was the 19th century," he said.

- "Cars?" I asked again.

- "No. That was the 20th century," he replied.

- "So?" I asked.

- "Cell phones and horses." Low-speed mobility with contextual information that emerges from mobile interfaces.

Incredible.

We travelled along rural roads near Centelles, close to Barcelona: I visited Mas Cerdà, which belonged to the family of Ildefons Cerdà, the engineer who, with a utopian vision for the construction of the human habitat, promoted the idea of "urbanizing" the countryside and "ruralizing" the city. And he invented the concept of urban design.

One hundred and fifty years later, we need to rewrite the history of human habitats.

Following page:
The Square Root House - Tiny Ecohouse: project of IaaC, developed at Master in Advanced Ecological Buildings in 2018/2019. Researchers: Pilar Aguirre, Giulia Astrachan, Jesús Carlos Bueno, Julianna Carmona, Vincent Charlebois, Yu-Wen Chen, Yu-Ching Chiang, Pablo Corroto, Nour El Kamali, Elisabet Fàbrega R.Roda, Kevin Matar, Jorge Luis Morales, Sinead Nicholson, Lian Qiao, Michael Salka, Yuanpei Tian, Zhipeng Yu, Jie Zhang, Heran Zu; Faculty: Vicente Guallart, Daniel Ibáñez, Marziah Zad.

Synthetic Landscapes

Claudia Pasquero, Marco Poletto
EcoLogicStudio

"[...] while we campaign to make our world 'cleaner' and less toxic, less harmful to sentient beings, our philosophical adventure should in some way be quite the reverse. We should be finding ways to stick around with the sticky mess that we are, making things dirtier, identify with ugliness [...]" Timothy Morton

The world we live in has often been obsessed with a search for truth from within a problem-solving framework. In our work, we wanted to discuss a way of approaching urban issues as a protocol of local interaction between human and non-human agents. For example, we are fascinated with a type of mold called Physarum polycephalum (slime mold), which many would consider as a biological computer. Representing a form of bio-artificial intelligence, slime mold is a unicellular organism consisting of millions of interacting nuclei, operating under the principle of collective intelligence. What emerges from these interactions can imitate sophisticated processes like network optimization and resource redistribution even at a low level.

What is interesting about slime mold is not its computational power, but rather the fact that computation can be embedded into matter. And as architects we wonder: Could this be embedded into an architectural medium? And, if so, what role can a microorganism such as slime mold have in architectural design? In our discipline, we inherited from modernity the idea that bacteria and micro-organisms are dangerous. Furthermore, modern master planning and modern design have strong roots in the concept of sanitation. Modernism embraced this attitude and turned it into a style. White clean surfaces came to symbolize humans' rational ability to frame nature and its darkest and uncontrollable aspects.

Modern master planning rationally separated all functions: zones of production and treatment of waste were moved further out of city centers, technically preventing a possible contamination of living quarters, but also removing the by-products of the urbanization from our sight and from our consciousness at a very fundamental level. This was the origin of the modern, industrialized and metabolically linear city. Modernity has not only sanitized our cities but also our understanding of what is natural versus what is artificial. Today we have a somewhat mechanical model of nature: not only what is natural is depicted as clearly separated from what is artificial but also our image of nature is dominated by ideal growth, prosperity and equilibrium.

We talk about re-greening cities and re-naturalizing forests as if such processes could lead to the re-equilibrium of the now temporarily perturbed biosphere. However, most natural and even artificial systems are non-linear and composed of billions of interlocking feedback loops; therefore, these processes of rebalancing require much more precision and accuracy.

Previous page:
BioTallinn, Anthropocene Island Photosynthetic Housing Perspective View North. Courtesy of Claudia Pasquero.

Processes such as destruction, death, decay, digestion and dissolution are some of the most fundamental to nature and a critical part of its circularity; these often take place in the dark, they generate strong odours, they trigger in us atavistic fears of contagion.

These processes constitute the dark face of ecology that we have all but erased from our consciousness and that is critical to the functioning of ecosystems. On the other hand, microorganisms have exceptional properties that we keep discovering in labs and that make them capable of turning what we consider pollution or waste into nutrients and raw materials; they could be the trigger to re-connect urban metabolisms to urban morphologies.

In this vision, fungi, microorganisms, machines and all other communication devices become, alongside human beings, bio-citizens, contributing to a sophisticated system of collective intelligence, the founding process for a new morphogenetic city.

This notion is key to one of our practice's longest-running projects, spanning an entire decade, called Urban Algae Farms. It is based on the idea of creating habitats for microalgae organisms as part of building envelopes. Within this framework, microalgae are not only able to photosynthesize but also to absorb emissions from the building itself. This new active layer becomes part of both the city and natural metabolic cycles, allowing green and dark ecologies to reconnect.

There are multiple interactions in buildings that can be activated by the intelligence of microalgae colonies. The microorganisms grow faster in our biomechanical environment than in the wild because they are very closely connected with the life of the building, and that stimulates their biomass to grow; the biomass can, in turn, be used by the inhabitants of the building itself as source of energy or food. It is a new kind of symbiosis. This means we start seeing buildings as something not necessarily finished at the end of construction; we understand that they can keep evolving. Our job is to imagine and design new urban typologies, new hybrid habitats for these emergent social groups.

We have just built an example of this in Astana, Kazakhstan called Bio.Tech Hut, our first permanent biotechnological dwelling. The Bio.Tech Hut is 180 sqm in plan, can host a large family, and supports 1600 l of living cultures of cyanobacteria in its lab-grade glass photo-bioreactors. In optimal conditions, it produces approx 1 kg of dry algae per day. Green microalgae can contain up to 60% oil, from which 1 kg of biofuel can be produced, releasing 10 KW/h of energy. That is enough to power an average UK home, which makes Bio.Tech Hut energetically self-sufficient. Yet, this principle of urban symbiosis must extend to food and nutrients; these are part of a crucial cycle, where important changes are required to feed a healthy diet to a growing urban population that is predicted to reach 5 billion in the next 15 years.

HORTUS_Astana: an art work produced for the bio-tech hut exhibition of Astana Expo 2017.

Tallinn Wet City, Green Network.
Courtesy of Claudia Pasquero.

Microalgae like Chlorella contains up to 60% vegetable proteins. Every day, the BIO.tech HUT produces up to 600 g of proteins, enough to supply the recommended daily intake for 12 adults. This is the equivalent in meat-based proteins of eight cows! And, of course, reducing farming also means reducing emissions of greenhouse gases. In optimal conditions, the living cultures of Chlorella growing within the BIO.tech HUT glass photo-bioreactors can absorb 2 kg of CO_2/day. That is equivalent of the CO_2 adsorbed by 32 large trees, which is equivalent to a family-run urban forest.

These numbers give us a spatial and material dimension of the efficiency of building integrated cultures and the urban fabric's ability to synthesize resources. It is a crucial transition, where the urban environment stops being just a container of programmes or functions – like the modern machine for living – and becomes a dynamic process of production, a living machine.

Our team at Photosynthetica recently promoted this vision with the curatorial project Anthropocene Island for TAB2017, which investigates the urban future of Tallinn, the capital of Estonia. The project site is a unique peninsula on the outskirts of Tallinn, a former Soviet military base that was abandoned after Estonia became an independent country. Nature and especially birds settled on it, as well as, more recently, the main wastewater treatment plant for Tallinn. Since then, a battle started among the plant management and ecologists claiming the plant is contaminating their reserve. It is a case of green vs. dark ecology; birds and bacteria, however, do not see it this way.

Following double page:
BioTallinn, Anthropocene Island Filtering Landscape.
Courtesy of Claudia Pasquero.

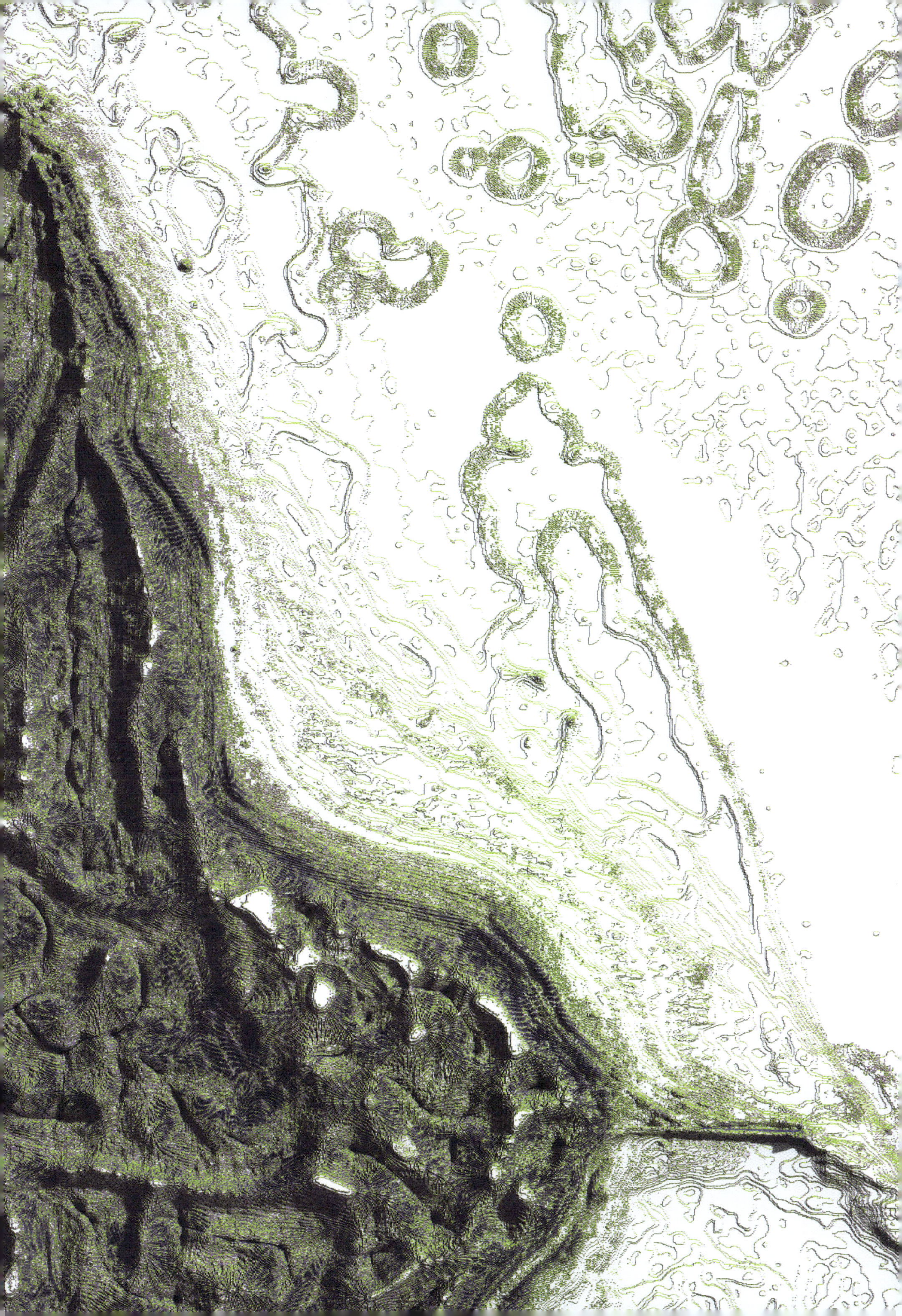

While the birds like the warm and nutritious water in the bio-digestion tanks and seem to play with its large machines, bacteria like Escherichia coli travel across the border of the waste water treatment plant via water percolation and into the nearby pond, making it one of the most eutrophied in Europe.

We decided to take the perspective of the birds and bacteria, a non-anthropocentric perspective, and we developed it into a speculative project that became the main exhibition at this year's Tallinn Architecture Biennale, conceived as a real laboratory of future city making. Here, we proposed a new city model that grows from the waste of Tallinn, integrating microorganisms into the built environment and exploring bio-digestion as a founding principle for a new city.

We proposed new distributed habitats with the capacity to receive Tallinn's wastewater, process it, generate heath and nutrients, host new species, increase photosynthesis, grow biomass, extract biofuel and feed it back to the city of Tallinn.

In this vision, birds, microorganisms, machines and all other communication devices become, alongside human beings, bio-citizens, contributing to a sophisticated system of collective intelligence, the founding process of a new metabolically circular bioTallinn. This speculative approach to ecological issues has led us to rethink climate change in a recent alpine project conducted with the Synthetic Landscape Lab and the University of Innsbruck.

The Alps as a topographic region recall idyllic portraits of unspoiled nature, featuring peaks, glaciers, lakes and pastures. Yet, perhaps paradoxically, the Alps are also a surprisingly potent reflection of the effects of climate change and of our conceptual and practical inability to deal with it.

Retreating glaciers are perhaps the most striking phenomenon of all; they are formations of geological time that are melting in front of our eyes in a matter of a few years. In their strata, literally frozen in time, is a repository of the alpine microclimate, recorded since before men ever set foot on them.

An enormous amount of data is stored in particles and molecules of air trapped in the layers of ice – every layer a year of history, a cycle of life. And we are all standing there and watching this all liquefy and vanish.

The project's aim has been to read and process this data before it disappears, seeking to materialize what climate change is from the perspective of the alpine ecosystem. We decoded these frozen dataspaces to unfold the anthropogenic dimension of alpine glaciers by drawing and simulating the complex web of relationships affecting their watersheds. Yearly cycles of freezing and melting have been modelled in their material, morphological and ecological actualization: water transitioning to snow, to ice and back to water, activating natural and man-made systems, from hydroelectric power plants, to tourist resorts, to pastoral communities.

A new computational alpine panorama appeared: a mathematical landscape where the true nature of glaciers was questioned, in the attempt to find a meaning for our Anthropocene Age unbiased by ideological posturing. From there, we progressed to actualize those abstract depictions on multiple scales, by testing ways in which we can affect the processes currently shaping glaciers' rapid decline and the consequent transformations occurring within their territory.

We have been intervening on multiple scales:
- the molecular scale, of particles and crystals;
- the mesoscale of pastoral communities, sky resorts and alpine cities;
- the macroscale of renewable energy networks, Europe's so-called Alpine Battery.

Our overarching goal has been to question (through drawings, models, prototypes, videos and installations) the material, morphological, social and exosystemic nature of climate change from the unique and specific perspective of an Alpine glacier.

Such questioning has global relevance, well beyond the specific aspects and solutions of our case study; and that is because the mediatic scaremongering tactics as well as the hard scientific evidence measured in centigrade and tons of CO_2, have failed in their ambition to create global consensus and trigger actions. On the contrary, they have contributed to a climate of increased ideological confrontation. Another tactic is necessary, other tools are required, and we are convinced that architects and urban designers have something to contribute here, with multidimensional, trans-disciplinary and ideologically unbiased depictions of the nature of climate change.

Innsbruck Synthetic Crystallization, Synthetic Crystallizations student model by Joy Boulois and Jens Burkart. Courtesy of Claudia Pasquero.

Innsbruck Synthetic Crystallization, Microscopic crystallization of ice from a student model by Manuel Perkmann and Emiliano Rando. Courtesy of Claudia Pasquero.

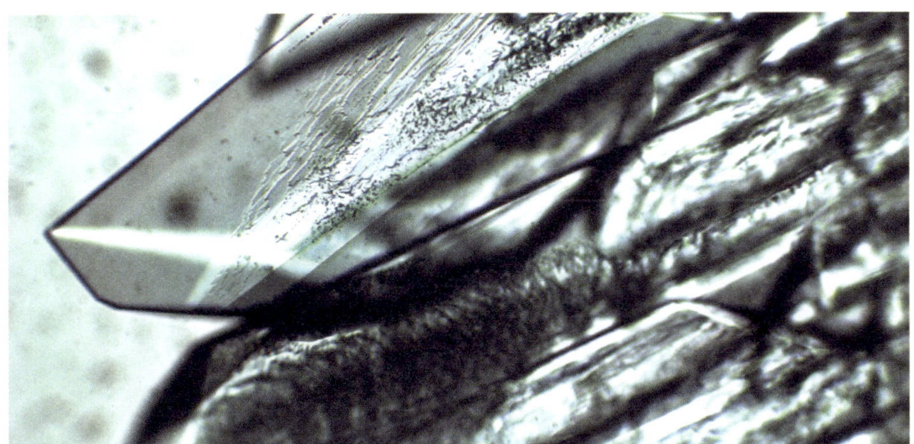

Following double page: Innsbruck Synthetic Crystallization, A computational alpine landscape drawing by Joy Boulois and Jens Burkart. Courtesy of Claudia Pasquero.

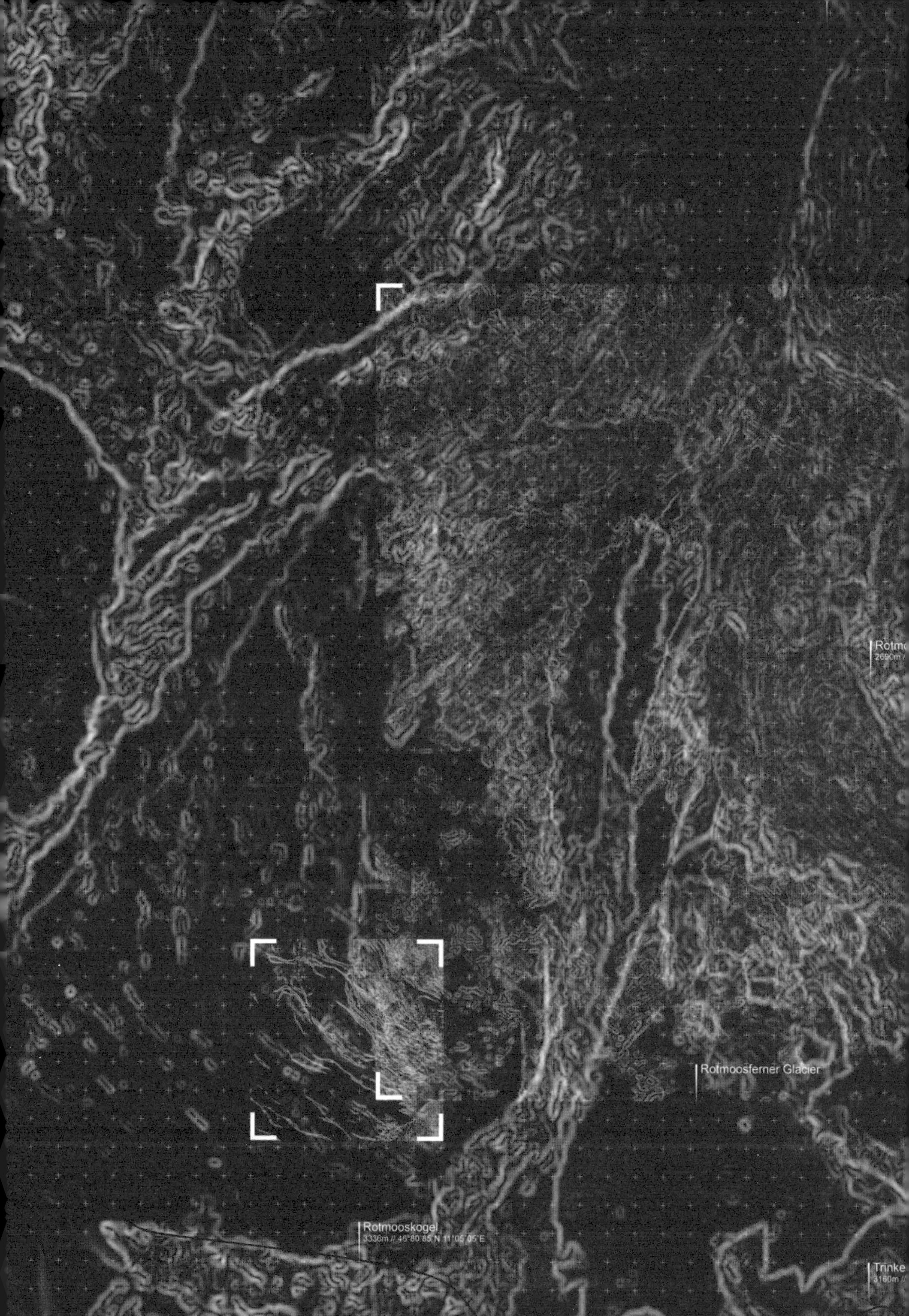

Rotmo
2690m /
Rotmoosferner Glacier
Rotmooskogel
3336m // 46°80'85'N 11°05'05'E
Trinke
3160m /

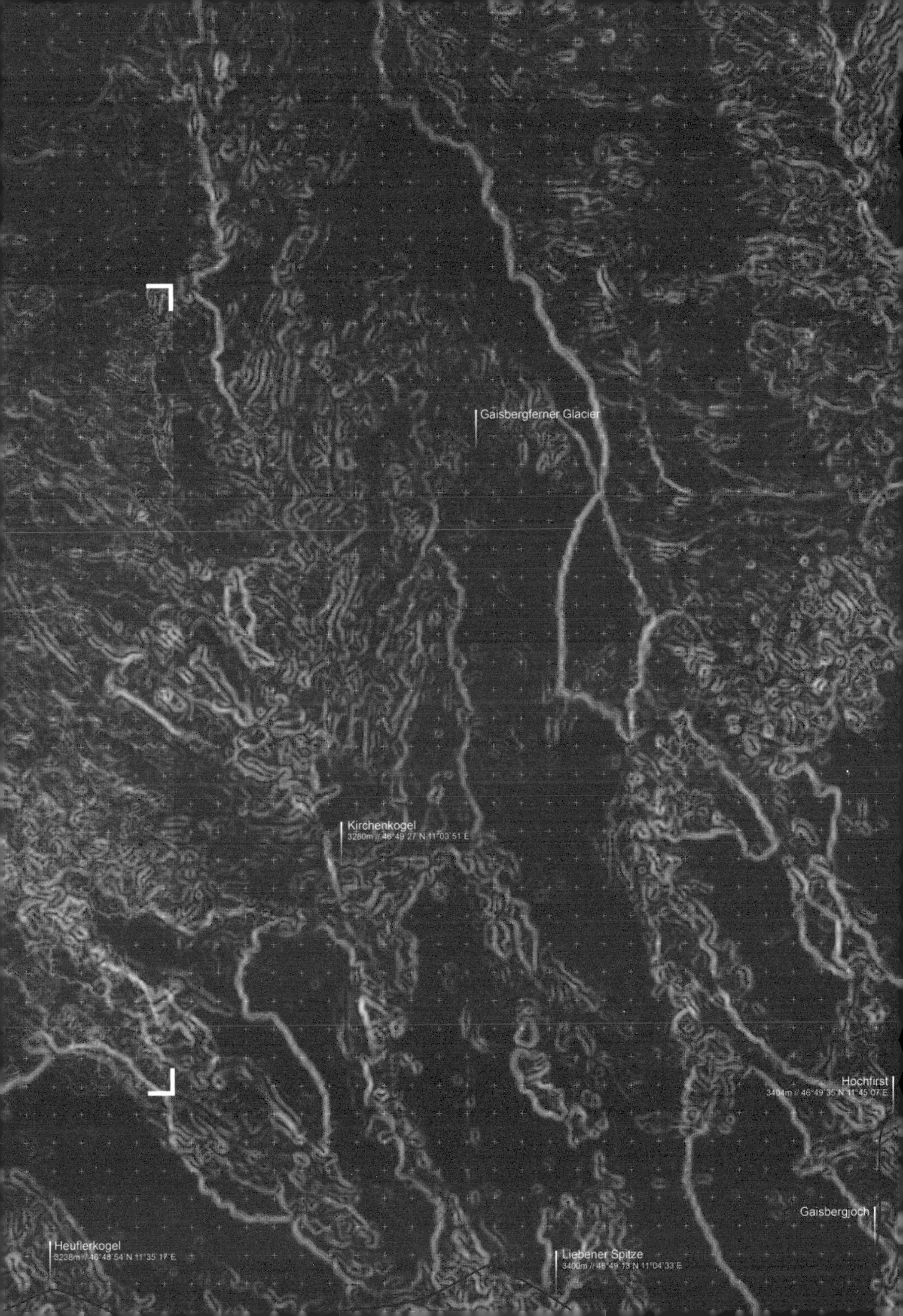

Gaisbergferner Glacier

Kirchenkogel
3280m // 46°49'27"N 11°03'51"E

Hochfirst
3404m // 46°49'35"N 11°45'07"E

Gaisbergjoch

Heuflerkogel
3238m // 46°48'54"N 11°35'17"E

Liebener Spitze
3400m // 46°49'13"N 11°04'33"E

Slow Crisis
Engineered Landscape Mutations

IAAC MAA/ Rodrigo Rubio, Ruxandra Iancu

Our current relentless planetary urbanization relies on a flawed modern ideal: one of a sharp detachment between human and non-human, between man-made systems and environmental dynamics, between economy and ecology.

The increasing unpredictability of hydrological, meteorological and geological patterns has revealed many of our serious vulnerabilities as builders and inhabitants of our own landscapes.[1]

This phenomenon is what we define as a 'slow crisis', whose pace and ungraspable scale seems to render it invisible for our human perspective. Slow Crisis is a research-based project that aims to build articulated operative knowledge on our current ecological transformations, their affects and effects on our urbanized world.

Following recent claims regarding the need for a contemporary redefinition of the term "infrastructure"[2] – soft rather than hard, environmentally resilient rather than mechanistically efficient, we will work on constructing a toolbox of engineered landscape mutations.

Research project of IaaC.
Developed at Master in Advanced Architecture 01 in 2016/2017. Faculty: Rodrigo Rubio, Ruxandra Iancu.

Previous page:
The Tagebau Garzweiler, a surface lignite mine in the German state of North-Rhine Westphalia.
Photo: Tobias Jussen on Unsplash.

Research Fields

We will continuously oscillate between the abstraction of synthetic analysis (data gathering, mapping, ecological modeling, etc.) and the concreteness of opportunistic strategies (detecting local material cultures and/or resources in order to activate ecological infrastructures), articulating the studies inside the following fields:

– Storms, sea-surface temperature rise, sea-level rise and coastal urban populations.
The continuous area along the coast that is less than 10 meters above sea level represents 2% of the world's land area but contains 10% of its total population (i.e., over 600 million people). Almost two-thirds of the world's cities with more than 5 million inhabitants fall in this zone.

Highly urbanized coasts most at risk therefore include Vietnam in Asia, Gujarat in western India and Orissa in eastern India, the Caribbean, including major urban settlements like Santo Domingo, Kingston and Havana, and those on Mexico's Caribbean coast and Central America.

– Floods and mudslides. Draught and erosion. Hydrological urban corridors.
The increasing unpredictability of meteorological patterns, together with uncontrolled processes of urbanization and land exploitation without a proper infrastructural layer, leads to fragile and nonresilient situations.

P.i. the floods in Mozambique in 2000, which included heavy floods in Maputo; heavy rains, floods and mudslides in East Africa in 2002, and the very serious floods in Port Harcourt and in Addis Ababa in 2006 (UN-Habitat 2007, Douglas et al., 2008).

P.i. the Hydrologic Corridor Project in Kenya by JustDigIt. During the last century, mean precipitation in all four seasons of the year has tended to decrease in all the world's main arid and semi-arid regions: Northern Chile, the Brazilian Northeast and Northern Mexico, West Africa and Ethiopia, the drier parts of Southern Africa, and Western China.

– Pollution and heat waves. Urban island effect.
Large metropolitan formations can generate an increase of near-surface temperature of two degrees over large regions, generating a feedback loop with humidity and pollutant formation.

Most cities in Africa, Asia, Latin America and the Caribbean will experience more heat waves. Many cities will face more problems with certain air pollutants as concentrations of air pollutants change in response to climate change, because a portion of their formation depends, in part, on temperature and humidity.

– Health risks and waste flows.
Deforestation, fast unregulated city growth, lack of proper sewage, drainage and waste collection, together with the expansion of tropical climates, leads to the emergence, urbanization and spread of diseases such as malaria, dengue and cholera.

Malaria is responsible for an estimated 300-500 million clinical attacks globally, and >1 million deaths each year, mainly among children under five years of age living in sub-Saharan Africa.

The disease accounts for an estimated loss of 44.7 million disability-adjusted life years (DALYs), more than 80% of which are currently concentrated in sub-Saharan Africa.

Short description of projects

Mumbai
Researchers: Valeria Julich, Ami Nigam, Mohamad Rachid Jalloul.

Deonar is a 90-year-old garbage dump situated between two living environments: one for humans, in a slum that lacks minimum living conditions; and the other for a dwindling population of mangroves, which used to be the major geo-characteristic of the once green archipelago, Mumbai. While the average age of a dumping ground is 40 years, Deonar was set up in 1927. There have been several legal attempts to close it, because it has been opened to the city's garbage for 90 years, accumulating waste as high as 18-story towers (70% of it is organic waste).

Toxic emissions and recurrent fires make the living situation very unhealthy for the people living in the adjacent slum. Shortages of water and electricity, and a lack of education worsen the situation in the slum. This turns the dump into the main source of a livelihood for many of the people living there – a matter that makes the closing even more complicated.

Mumbai, once a seven-island archipelago, has most of its current area reclaimed from the sea, a large-scale engineering feat undertaken by the British in the 19th century. This led to the massive deforestation of mangroves – trees with rich ecological benefits including water and atmospheric quality improvement, sea-level control and shoreline protection from erosion. In turn, apart from the monsoon season, the city has been facing yearly major floods that generate an environment for the transmission of diseases like smallpox, cholera, plague, scarlet fever and malaria. Understanding the three major components of this intensifying social, waste and ecological crisis, the solution proposes an archaeological excavation of the almost century-old trash dump by digging inverted pyramids reminiscent of India's step wells.

In these open mine structures, the process is divided into three steps: unearthing, sorting and fabricating. Depending on the type of waste sorted, it can provide a range of uses, from handicrafts to building materials. As more waste is unearthed, the wells go deeper to tap into the water that will reclaim the land, giving back the mangroves their environment.

Open mine structures to unearth waste. Mumbai project.

Traffic, pollution, conflicts, corruption... but what was the straw that broke the camel's back? The Trash Crises.

After the Naameh landfill was closed by the residents living nearby, the streets of Beirut were drowned by garbage. This drastic situation lasted for several months. The government stood idly by until people lost their patience and Beirut's streets were then filled with protesters starting riots.

The project proposal tackles this problem by adopting a strategy that will solve much more than the garbage crisis: a strategy that implies different scales, starting from the neighborhood and reaching the territorial scale. This strategy involves the electricity crisis that has been affecting the country as a whole since 1990 (post-war era). The intention is to find common strategic solutions, where one problem can become the solution to another and vice-versa.

Beirut
Researchers: Maria Sfeir, Zina Alkhani, Antoun Rizk.

Following page:
Abandoned power plants near Beirut: interventions in these areas, to use the garbage, specifically organic waste, as fuel to generate energy, and creating greener spaces through composting. Beirut project.

Informal settlements invading Rafik Harriri International Airport, one of the problems of the city of Beirut. Beirut project.

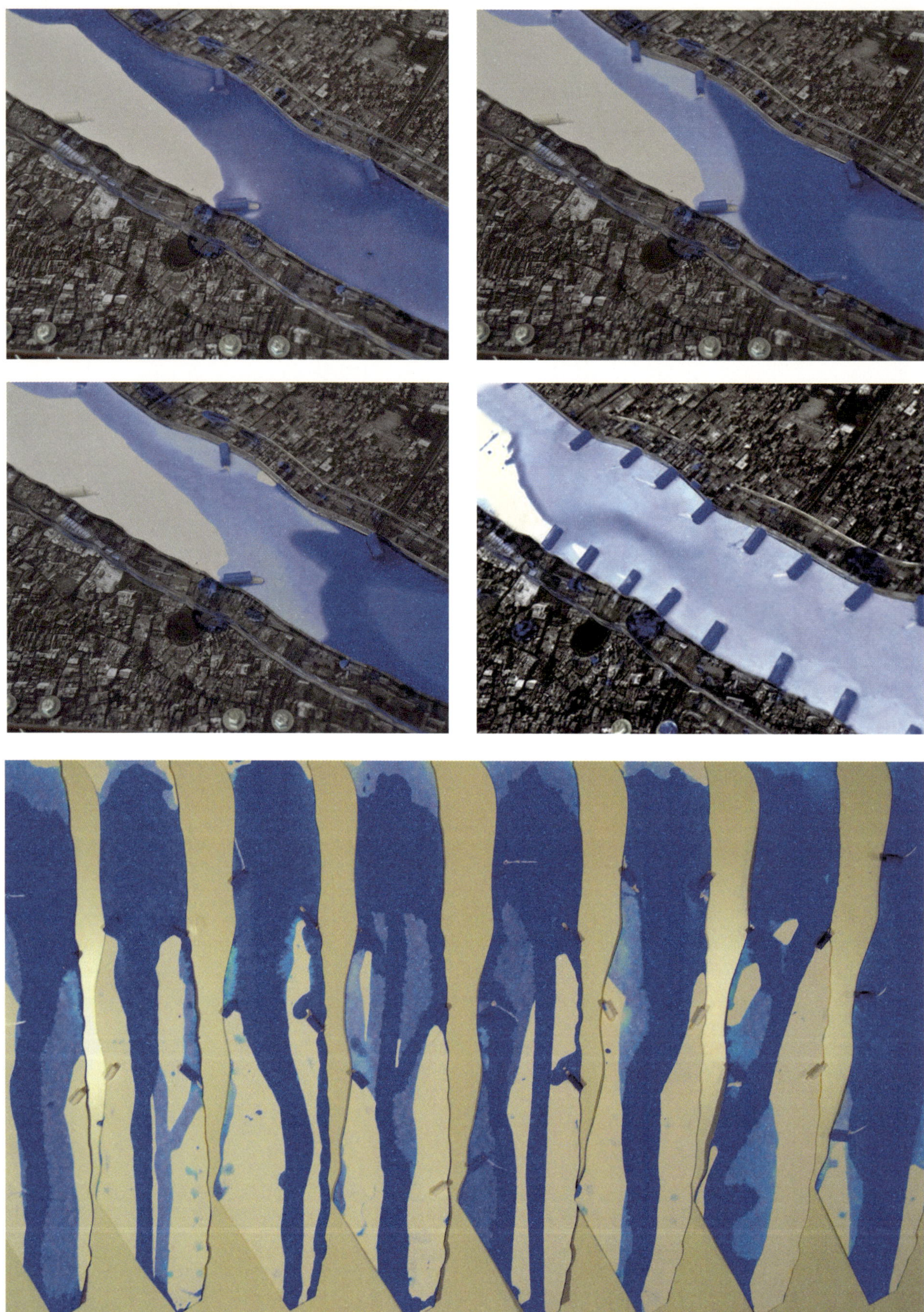

Dhaka
Researchers: Abraham Ninan, Sheikh Rizvi Riaz.

Previous page:
Context of the project and test analysing the flow of Buriganga river and creating interventions to divert the sediments into predetermined locations. Dhaka project.

Test analysing the flow of Buriganga river and creating interventions to divert the sediments into predetermined locations. Dhaka project.

The slow crisis affecting the city of Dhaka is the flooding of the Buriganga River. This impacts people's lives in a very devastating way and also causes a scarcity of greenery and vegetation in the city. The rising sea level on one hand, and the melting of the ice caps in the Himalayas where the river originates on the other, are the cause of this seasonal flooding. One positive aspect of this flooding, however, is that the river brings exceptionally fertile soil from the plains of the Himalayas.

The proposal aims at controlling this flooding and using it to enhance the city. By analyzing the flow of the river and by creating interventions, the sediments will be diverted into predetermined locations. These locations will be designed to become the green areas that the city needs, which will also enhance the biodiversity of the region.

The Proposed Green Belt will work as a closed loop system tying all the activities together. It includes waste water treatment, fuel generation, fertilizer production, energy production and supply of fire wood and building material. Tree plantations along the banks to increase and improve the natural levee can be an important aspect for the sustainability of the river area, which can also protect from land erosion and flooding during the rainy season.

The flooding of the Buriganga river. Image based on CFD (Computational fluid dynamics). Dhaka Project.

New Orleans

Researchers: Jihan Shraibati, Mohamad Al Chawa, Mubashir Jabir

Located on the Southern coast of the United States, New Orleans (or NOLA as it is referred to by inhabitants) is defined by its various rivers, bayous, lakes, and swamps, including the Mississippi River and Lake Pontchartrain to the North. These bodies of water have become one of the major economic centers for the nation and have made the city the sixth-largest port in the United States by volume of cargo.

Culturally, NOLA is most well known for its jazz, its creole cuisine, and the large, annual celebration of Mardi Gras. On a national level, the city provides a major source of imports, including petrochemicals, coal, coffee and steel. Climatically, the city is infamous for its frequent and devastating hurricanes and high flood seasons, which are a constant challenge to infrastructure; natural and human-induced subsidences continue to lower many areas of the city below sea level, creating a bowl effect that enhances floodwaters and contributes to the devastation of natural disasters, specifically hurricanes. These almost annual phenomena are a natural process that is greatly shaping the urban environment of the city, from the small to the large scale.

This study is an attempt to, first, understand the existing nature and conditions of the city in climatic definitions and, second, to provide an anthropogenic solution for treating these climatic shifts.

The nature of urban expansion and the destruction of wetlands led to the catastrophic damages from Hurricane Katrina in 2005. Though the city is a veteran of hurricanes, and Katrina was not the most damaging by far, poor infrastructure upkeep, a disregard of building code guidelines, the breach of levees, and bowl-affect flooding all combined into a devastating impact.

As shown by the satellite images from 2004 to 2009, the water-to-land ratio has increased significantly. While the City of New Orleans is taking steps to rectify this land loss, solutions are being enacted slowly.

Therefore, a new, multi-layered approach is necessary to study, set up and design a plan that will be viable financially, and effective permanently.

This proposal aims to use natural water flows to restore the vital ecological systems of the surrounding area, thus preventing further damage, while simultaneously harvesting hydro-energy, wind energy, and piezo-energy from nature.

References:

1. Carlson, Dane. "The humanity of infrastructure. Landscape as operative ground". In *Scenario Journal,* nr. 3 - Rethinking Infrastructure (Spring 2013).

2. Belanger, Pierre. "Redefining Infrastructure". In *Ecological Urbanism*, edited by Mostafavi and Doherty. Baden: Lars Muller Publishers, 2010.

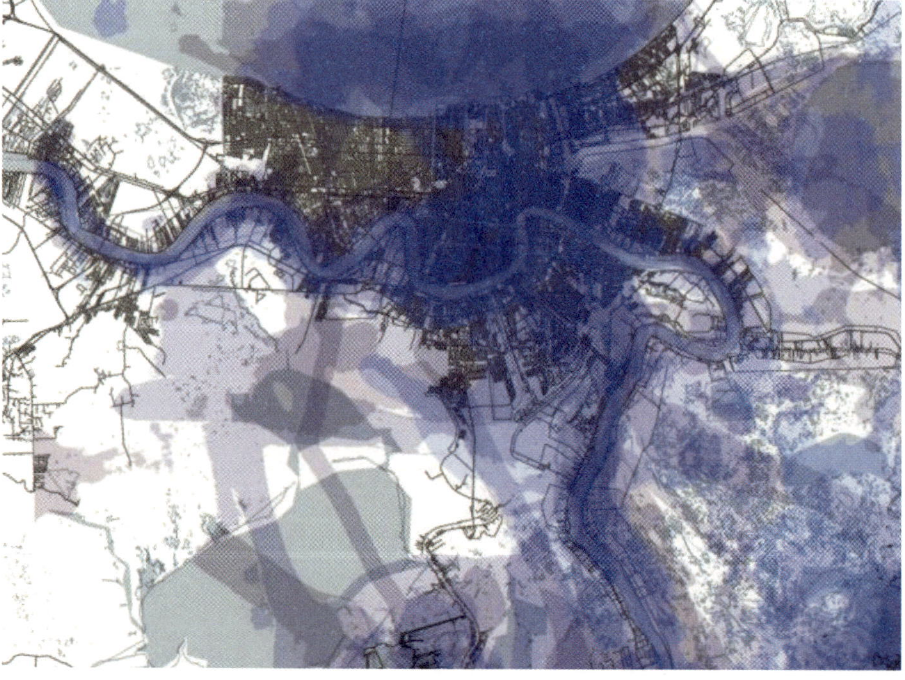

Analogue Studies overlay. New Orleans project.

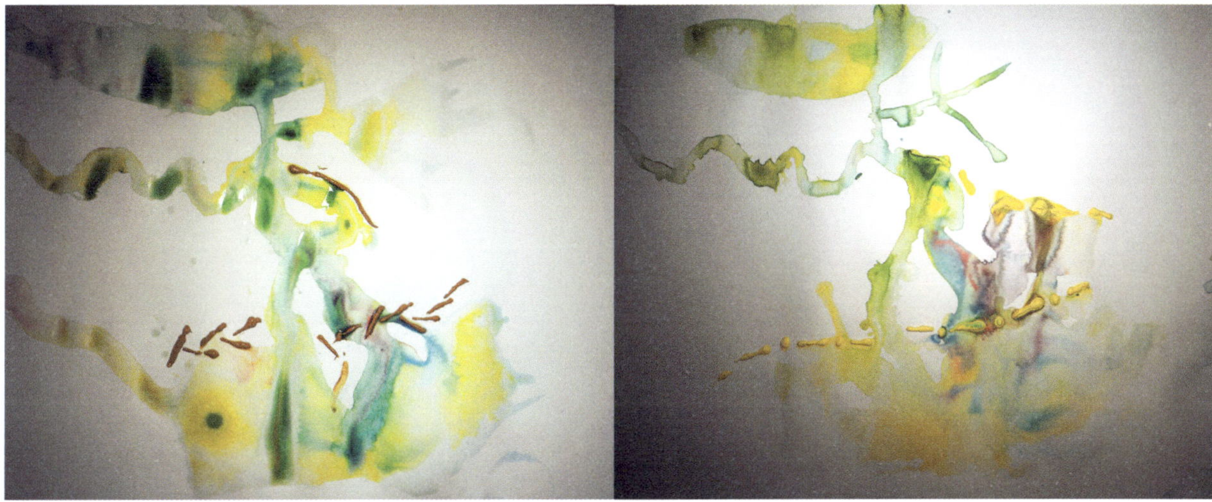

Analogue Studies for flood patterns (pigment on paper). New Orleans project.

Following double page:
Surrealistic industrial lake in Poland. Sony World Photography Awards 2017 Shortlist. Photo: Mariusz Prusaczyk on Unsplash.

Nikel. Dark Materiality of an Arctic city

Katya Larina, Tatjana Gorbachewskaya

We explore the phenomena of the remote industrial mining settlement of Nikel (named after the material mined there), through the lens of the unique material substances that have emerged there.

Our research presents the material as a real and symbolic element that represents both the creation and subsequent decline of the city.

We draw a parallel between the history of the town and the history of the man-made material.

The history of both illustrates the transformation of our ideas about the limits of the artificial world we create on Earth.

Nikel is an extreme experiment of a large industrial town built beyond the Arctic circle, which reflects both the utopian socialist ideology and the nation's optimism in attempting to conquer the unknown landscapes of the north.

It was built as part of a greater infrastructure dedicated to serving the mining industry of the Soviet Union. As this infrastructure was neglected, Nikel was left on its own both to fight the harsh arctic climate of the Murmansk region and to manage the socio-economic crisis of the post-Soviet period. Today, Nikel is an example of one link in a chain of mono-functional cities resulting from the former Soviet/ contemporary Russian industrial machine.

Previous page:
An example where industrial byproducts of the smelting industry became one of the "local" materials: slag was one of these and has been used for the insulation filling inside walls. The slag, in contact with the mortar in the wall structure, had acquired incredible strength, so the buildings cannot be demolished and even today few of them stand in the city empty and partially destroyed.

Nikel forms its own unique ecology. As it was brought into the Arctic environment as an alien component, the city had to either import all the materials it was built with – or create its own. Due to the extreme enclosure of the settlement, the materiality of Nikel is formed from the by-products of its principal industrial activity.

Here, the industrial byproducts – or, as we call them, the 'dark' components of the material world of the city – are not hidden and ignored but rather the opposite; they are exposed and, in some ways, utilized.

We borrowed the term relating to the dark side of the material world from the concept of "dark ecology", coined by Timothy Morton. In his book *The Ecological Thought* (2010), he shows that the ecological thought is not nice and green and a celebration of all things natural.

Morton writes:

"It would make more sense to design in a dark ecological way, admitting our coexistence with toxic substances we have created and exploited".[1]

In Nikel, we can observe how "dark" components of the material world became a building material for the city, penetrating the physical material of the city on a variety of levels.

In our research, we will present some of the "dark" materials we discovered there and will investigate, on a micro scale, their physical properties, and on a macro scale, the socio-economic processes they triggered, as well as the environmental processes in the region.

Nikel, artificial environment, city under the dome

Built in an area of extreme living conditions, the city of Nikel appeared as an artificial organism covered by a top-down intangible protective dome, consisting of vital infrastructure and, importantly, of careful management of that infrastructure over many years by the state. It became a great example of cities that were alienated from the natural environment and climate, constituting a new world in themselves.

In the Soviet period of the development of the city, the relationship to nature was focused on glorifying the conquest of nature, as seen in the desire to modernize and construct a better environment for living.

Dedicated to fighting natural conditions, Nikel was totally dependent on a single monopolist – the state – not only as an employer, but also as a supplier of all resources, including the most basic commodities.

The whole logic of the city construction was considered in terms not of the natural climatic condition, but as an artificially constructed environment. In our research, we came across an image on the cover of *Young Technician*, a Soviet magazine published in the 1980s.

The image was a fantasy about the Soviet northern settlement, represented as a series of Fuller-like domes connected by passages.

This futuristic image of the settlement somehow inspired us to draw a parallel between the story of the city and the post-Uexküll understanding of the environment, perceived as "not just the natural habitat of exotic animals and plants but also the procedures for the technical reproduction of that habitat in alien surroundings".[2]

The constructed *Umwelt* (the environment or surroundings) forms a figurative "bubble" around the city, "inside" of which certain things are significant and meaningful, and "outside" of which other things are as good as nonexistent insofar as they are "hidden in infinity".[3]

In turn, Nikel also became a place that could be artificially and technologically reproduced anywhere – a place that denies its environment, no longer related to its geological or climatic context.

The toxic copper-nickel dust, the slag, which forms black dunes and which spreads over the vast territory, contaminating the local ecology. Annually, Nikel's industry produces 1.35 million tonnes of this toxic dust.

The philosopher Sloterdijk both appropriates and reforms the contour of Uexküll's ethological bubble, suggesting "that the human is, first, a privileged sphere-maker, but that, at the same time, the human is also passively acted upon by an outside".[4]

As an element of the big Soviet industrial machine, the city was shaping its own "sphere", its own closed system of life-support infrastructure, ready to fight and resist but not to collaborate with the arctic. During those years, Nikel developed a set of infrastructural elements of resistance, such as artificial daylight to resist the polar winter darkness and a network of central heating to withstand the cold climate. This process of exchanging materials and energy, functioning and failing to function, is captured in the physical form of the city's infrastructure.

Also, the city enjoyed a highly subsidized social infrastructure, which attracted people to live and work there despite the extreme climatic conditions. It was a unique experiment for a city that had the northernmost collective farm, the northernmost zoo, the northernmost railway station, a cultural palace, art school and so on.

The city of Nikel provided a range of "good-climate" factors, such as a high pensions, double holiday time, earlier retirement, and good facilities for sport and education.

Nikel became one of the "spheres" or, more precisely, to use the terminology of Russian thinker Vladimir Vernadsky, one of the "technospheres" engineered by the state to function as part of the bigger industrial machine of the Soviet colonization of Siberia and the North. According to Vernadsky, the new environments constructed by men (in contrast to natural systems) often exceed the simple need for survival. Human expansion "occurs simultaneously in two directions: first, by unlocking worlds previously foreclosed to the human senses through the development of intrusive technological means; and, second, by expediting the growth of specific worlds by fantastically augmenting the distribution of their material components to create apparently advantageous conditions for the expansion of the human species".[5]

Dark materials of Nikel

In the Soviet period, the government strictly required the use of local materials for construction, and industrial byproducts from the smelting industry became one of the "local" materials.

The city became an experimental plant for testing a variety of applications for these industrial substances, without a clear understanding of the danger and consequences that the presence of these often toxic materials would entail. One of them is copper-nickel dust, the slag that forms black dunes and spreads over the vast territory, contaminating the local ecology.

Annually, Nikel's industry produces 1.35 million tons of this toxic dust. These dunes of black slag spread over a territory of 84 hectares around the city and, at their highest, exceed 15 meters in height.

Dispersed by the prevailing winds towards the settlement, the sharp black crystals of slag cut into the surfaces of the town, accumulating in cracks between materials and penetrating through the surfaces.

Black dust mixed with the brightly painted surfaces of the city (which are, in turn, required to reduce the color starvation of the citizens) creates a specific texture inherent to most of the buildings in the town. In Nikel, slag has been widely used as a material for public spaces or housing elsewhere.

For instance, it has been used as an anti-slip substance on icy roads or as the finishing material for the football stadium.

The "dark" substance became a building material for the city, an inherent component of the artificial environment Nikel created within its "technosphere".

There are many examples in the city where slag has been used for the insulation filling inside walls. Over time, the slag came into in contact with the mortar in the wall structure and revealed new properties. The slag acquired incredible strength, so the buildings could not be demolished. Even today, a few of them are still standing in the city, empty and only partially destroyed.

Another example of the application of the byproducts of the Nikel smelting industry was the use of so-called phyllite. In that period, the local concrete factory used it as a filling material in concrete panels for prefabricated housing structures.

The filling material was approved without testing. A couple of years later, unexpected chemical reactions started to take place, and the concrete panels used for the construction of the buildings started bursting from the inside. The result is an unusual façade pattern in the city, where the walls are partially rebuilt with bricks or show cracks that are filled in with brick bands.

"Dark materials" existed in so many forms in the city: as a physical by-product of industrial activity, and as materials affected by industrial processes, such as stone or wood eroded by acid rain. All these dark materials modified and formed the new environment of the city from its internal resource: nickel. The city of Nikel was recycling and utilizing the materials it produced, partially because of the efficiency but also driven by the optimistic idea of inventing a new world out of new man-made materials.

The image of this new world prevailed, leaving behind the reality of the true physical properties of these alien materials. All these non-standard, unknown construction materials were utilized in the conventional forms of the standardized designs of Soviet modernist architecture. Built on an industrial scale following the principles of mass production, Nikel followed standards and regulations that were inadequately adjusted to the local conditions.

These regulations were developed and applied in state planning bureaus, which were often ill-informed about the reality of the arctic conditions and ignorant of the real environmental data or the physical qualities of the materials. All the new materials and byproducts generated by the internal resources of the city were applied in a utilitarian way, following abstract codes and regulations. They had been treated as passive matter, without considering the material's true properties and capacities.

Eventually, the dark materials revealed all of their hidden properties, transforming the natural ecology and the city itself from the inside.

Catastrophe

As the level of smelting production reached its peak in the 1970s, the sulfur from the highly enriched ore imported to Nikel from Eastern Siberia caused environmental catastrophe, as the acid rain deforested all of the area around the city. This was soon followed by the socio-economic catastrophe caused by the collapse of the Soviet Union. Political and economic change led to the loss of the power of the state over the industry and the city, and the consequential loss of the protective dome that had been built and maintained from the top down throughout the settlement's existence.

During the economic crisis of the 1990s, intense streetlights, which were meant to compensate for the lack of natural light during the polar winter, worked only during limited hours.

The city dwellers then felt a deficit of light and were greatly affected by it. In addition, poor maintenance and either unstable or frozen ground caused the central heating (which had initially been hidden underground) to become exposed on the surface, forming an intertwined three-dimensional landscape and emphasizing the city's artificiality.

Slavoj Žižek claims that "A lesson we should all learn from good Darwinists like Stephen Gould is that nature is not a balanced totality, which then we, humans, disturb.

Nature is a series of unimaginable catastrophes".[6]

When the artificial environment of the city of Nikel, maintained from the top down for so many years, became neglected, all the synthetic materials that had been under its protective dome were exposed not only to the arctic climate of the Murmansk region but additionally to the conditions of the post-Soviet socio-economic crisis. After the loss of its protective dome, the materials of the closed system of Nikel slowly started the process of redistribution and developed some form of interaction with the surrounding ecology, thereby taking on new qualities: qualities of an open system able to communicate and adapt.

In the abandoned parts of the city of Nikel, where the natural processes of ecological competition occur, we discovered that a variety of ecological patches appeared within the scale of a single building, a single flat or an urban block.

There, the materials and matter either resist each other or form a variety of hybrids of multi-material samples. This brought us back to the concept of the bubble Uexküll proposed, where he says:

> "We must first blow a soap bubble around each creature to represent its own world, filled with the perceptions which it alone knows. When we ourselves step into one of these bubbles, the familiar meadow is transformed. Many of its colourful features disappear, others no longer belong together but appear in new relationships".[7]

The reference to individual soap bubbles helps us to illustrate the process of disruption and restructuring of the broken ecology of Nikel. The city contained in one "technosphere" by centralized control turned into a 'soap bubble' foam of interacting patches and environments, mobilizing all the available resources, dynamically changing, disappearing and multiplying.

Under the pressure of the extreme conditions, materials not only decay but also evolve more rapidly.

All the elements of the environment, living and nonliving, are forced to interact and cooperate with each other, forming new hybrid ecologies in order to survive. Materials also change their properties and appearance, mix and blend, redistributing and joining their energy and forces, acquiring a multi-material property. This multi-materiality may discover "a hidden dimension of material existence" of the dark materials that appeared in Nikel.[8] The dark substances the city generated, such as slag and phyllite, have always been perceived as materials with fixed properties.

Black dust mixed with the brightly painted surfaces of the city creates a specific texture inherent to most of the buildings in the town. The sharp black crystals dispersed by the prevailing winds into the surfaces of the town, are accumulating in cracks between materials and penetrating through the surfaces.

Within the process of liberation of those materials from the borders of the artificial ecology of Nikel, and the dynamic mixture and interaction of materials caused by the failure of the "protective dome" of the technosphere, the properties and new dimensions of the existence of the "dark" materials are being revealed. Over time, under these processes, local micro-organisms and plants are developing forms of symbiosis with such dark substances, one example of which is the copper-nickel dust.

The black dunes of toxic ashes became covered by green layers of plants and fungus, showing the power of organic matter to continuously accumulate the energy to live. Here, we can observe the symbiosis of naturally self-evolving interrelationships between dark materials and natural components. On the local scale of microorganisms, we can also see how natural ecology slowly restores itself, absorbing and setting up a new co-existence with the alien substance of the Nikel artificial ecology.

There is a still an open question regarding how this symbiosis may be achieved on the larger scale of the socio-economic and environmental interaction of the broken "technosphere" of the city and the natural ecology of the Arctic.

Nickel as a physical material and as a symbolic notion penetrates all the levels of the settlement's existence, representing the evolution of the artificial, city-created ecology. At first, there was nickel – the material was the reason the settlement was built, then there was the use of nickel's by-products for the city's construction, nickel's subsequent devastation of the local ecology as a result of the acid rain and slag it generated, and finally the symbiosis of copper-nickel dust with local microorganisms. The story of the material is interconnected with the life cycle of the city itself, its rise and fall. Within the lifetime of the settlement, through the wide spectrum of new materials, the natural resource hidden underground has formed a thick layer of "dark" topography, seamlessly merged with the natural landscape on both a micro and macro scale.

As the level of smelting production reached its peak in the 1970s. the sulfur from the highly enriched ore from Eastern Siberia imported to Nikel, caused environmental catastrophe as the acid rain deforested all of the area around the city.

Considering nickel's multi-materiality, acquired over all the time of its existence, it is impossible to draw the line anymore between what has been made by humans and what by natural ecology.

Slavoj Žižek, in the interview he gave in front of the trash plant, says "This is where we should start feeling at home...in our daily perception, the reality is that this disappears from our world... But the problem is that trash doesn't disappear.[9]

He indicates the ideological habit that a certain part of our material reality is vanishing from our daily perception.

In oppose to that in Nikel dark materials has a strong presence. Our research will suggest that, rather than seeing these by-products as being inherently negative, these by-products can have unintended impacts. Once introduced, they become part of the new ecology and need to be recognized as such.

Talking about ecology without nature, Slavoj Žižek says: "The ultimate obstacle to protecting nature is the very notion of nature we rely on".[10] Consequently, we are not only interested in the failed past of human ambition to overcome nature; our aim is also to discover the processes of evolution of the dark materials driven by both human ambition and also the forces of the natural environment, which together shape the existing and future landscape of the post-human ecology of the Arctic.

References:

1. Morton, Timothy. Unsustaining, online publication at http://www.worldpicturejournal.com/WP_5/Morton.html, 2011.

2. Sloterdijk, Peter. "Atmospheric Politics". In *Making Things Public: Atmospheres of Democracy* (Translated from German by Jeremy Gaines), edited by Latour and Weibel: MIT Press (2005), p. 947.

3. Buchanan, Brett. " Jakob von Uexküll's Theories of Life ". In *Onto-Ethologies. The Animal Environments of Uexkull, Heidegger, Merleau-Ponty, and Deleuze.* Albany: State University of New York Press (2008), p. 10.

4. Turpin, Etienne. " A Stroll Through the Bubbles of Chemicals and Men". In *Volume* magazine, nr. 35 (2013), pp. 42-49.

5. Ogurtsov, Alexander. "The history of science as a way to Noosphere: the concept of Vernadsky". In the Electronic philosophical journal *Vox / Голос*, nr. 17 (December 2014), pp 15-16.

6. Taylor, Astra. *Examined life: Excursions with contemporary thinkers.* New York: The New Press (2009), p. 112.

7. Von Uexküll, Jakob. "A Stroll Through the Worlds of Animals and Men". In *Instinctive Behavior: The Development of a Modern Concept*, translated and edited by Claire H. Schiller. New York: International Universities Press, Inc., p. 5.

8. Malafouris, Lambros. "Multi-materiality", Lecture at the Symposium Future Matters: The Imminent Reality of Multi-materiality. AASchool, London (2015).

9. Altena, Arie. Dark Ecology reading list (http://www.darkecology.net/dark-ecology-reading-list), 2014, p. 114.

10. Reaed C. and Lister N.M. *Projective ecologies.* Harvard University Graduate school of design: Actar (2014), p. 85.

The Monarch Sanctuary

Terreform ONE

In his influential book, *Architecture of the Well-Tempered Environment* (1969), Reyner Banham examined the dynamic history of mechanization in human habitats. This anthropocentric viewpoint addressed how space was transformed by artificial systems of heat-ing, ventilation, cooling, or lighting. Now, building energy use is per-haps the central problem in climate change. In the United States alone, 40% of all energy goes into mechanical systems for homes and offices. Banham's book sought to establish a new paradigm: what we call ecological architecture today.

Perhaps more importantly, it an-ticipated the radical shift from architecture for human populations towards architecture as an environmental practice. Given the enormous impact of the built sector on the ecosystem, architecture is no longer about the modernist production of space or form but rather a total all-encompassing environment.

Client: Kenmare Square LLC. Jackie Jangana and Andrew Kriss
Team: Terreform ONE
Principals: Mitchell Joachim, Christian Hubert; Project Architect: Nicholas Gervasi, Kristina Goncharova, Yucel Guven, Zhan Xu; Research: Larissa Belcic, Shahira Hammad, Deniz Onder, Aleksandr Plotkin, Tech Consultant: Anouk Wipprecht; Sponsor: Intel.

Previous page:
Facade axonometry. Courtesy of Joachim Mitchell.

The massive changes in climate dynamics, apparent in recent decades (since the first measurement of the Keeling Curve in 1958), make us question the division between the man-made and the natural environment, between man versus nature. While it was an optimistic sign of progress at the onset of the Industrial Revolution, this divide is no longer productive, and perhaps outright dangerous. In fact, the entire argument shifts towards the socio-ecological realm, which affects humankind as well as fauna and flora. Our planet is in the midst of its sixth wave of extinction in the past half a billion years. This is the worst increment in the loss of plant and animal species since the disappearance of the dinosaurs 65 million years ago. Architecture needs to be designed for the other 99% of species on the planet. Mass extinction has led to thinking about architecture for other organisms. As a counter move, we would like to propose a comprehensive strategy for the preservation of species through the built realm. This means putting other life forms first. The dialogue about the opposition or the union between man and nature is by no means new. Its idyllic narratives can be found in the Bible among other sources. On the purest level, this theoretical frame seeks to redefine the idea of the Garden of Eden. Eden can be considered the first landscape designed by divine will for humans, as well as animals and plants – a metaphor for a sanctuary where humankind was in harmony with nature. Eden is a phenomenological state, and perhaps unattainable. Yet its percepts are one of clearest for dwelling in congruence with all creatures of the Earth.

The resultant socio-ecological research and design initiative is ded-icated to raising awareness of the inevitability of massive environ-mental shifts and climate change as a consequence of human activity. Our goal is to develop an audit of all extinct species and to recreate an environmental framing for each organism. The project includes those organisms already on the Red List, as well as those that may become a part of it in the immediate future.

The project

The Monarch Sanctuary (*Lepidoptera terrarium*) will be eight stories of new commercial construction in Nolita, NYC. Programmatically, the building space will mostly contain retail and office life. Yet, central to its purpose is serving as a breeding ground and sanctuary for the monarch butterfly (*Danaus plexippus*). It is a pioneering building – one that aims to be ecologically generous, weaving butterfly conservation strategies into its design through the integration of monarch habitat in its façades, roof and atrium. Not just a building envelope, the edifice is a new biome of coexistence for people, plants and butterflies.

The monarch butterfly of North America is a threatened species. The U.S. Fish & Wildlife Services is currently assessing whether the monarch needs to be granted "endangered species" status, while the monarch population erodes due to the combined forces of agricultural pesticides and habitat loss. Monarchs are a delicate presence in New York City, migrating each year from Mexico and Florida to the city's precious green spaces to lay their eggs on the milkweed plant.

This project will vitally serve as a large-scale Lepidoptera terrarium. It will bolster the monarch's presence in the city through two strategies: open plantings of milkweed and nectar flowers on the roof, rear façade, and terrace will provide a breeding ground and habitat for wild monarchs; while enclosed colonies in the atrium and on the street-side double-skin façade will support the monarch population. The insects will be periodically released to join the wild population, enhancing overall species population numbers.

Our connection the community of NYC is essential. The prime location will attract attention and educate the public on Monarch extinction. It has a total area of 30,000 square feet and is to be located in the heart of Nolita, between Soho and the burgeoning art district along the Bowery, and a few blocks west of the New Museum. The site is just around the corner from the Storefront for Art and Architecture and currently exists as two plots occupied by small residential buildings, which will be combined into a single property.

Following page:
Exterior double-skin street facade: "vertical meadow," as an incubator and safe haven for Monarchs.
Courtesy of Joachim Mitchell.

Following page:
Top: Monarch Sanctuary in the context of Monarch migrations. Courtesy of Joachim Mitchell.

Bottom: Energy Diagram: the building is intended to serve as an object lesson in enhancing the urban environment with green technologies.
Courtesy of Joachim Mitchell.

Although it is a relatively small commercial building by New York standards, the building will present a striking public face and a powerful argument in favor of a diversity of life forms in the city. It will face Petrosino Square, a small triangular paved public park, named after a fallen NYPD lieutenant. The façade of the Monarch Sanctuary building will add a lush vertical surface to the edge of the square.

The double-skin street façade, with a diagrid structure of in-filled glass on the outer layer and with "pillows" of EFTE foil on the inner layer, encloses a careful climate-controlled space, three feet deep and seven stories tall. This "vertical meadow," the terrarium proper, serves as an incubator and safe haven for Monarchs in all seasons. It contains suspended milkweed vines and flowering plants to nourish the butterflies at each stage of their life cycle. Hydrogel bubbles on the EFTE help maintain optimal humidity levels, and sacs of algae help purify the air and the building's wastewater. Solar panels on the roof provide renewable energy to assist in powering the facilities.

Other features of the project are equally in service of the insects. LED screens at the street level provide magnified live views of the caterpillars and butterflies in the vertical meadow, which also connects to a multi-story atrium adjacent to the circulation core. Interior partitions are constructed from mycelium, and additional planting on the ceiling enhances the interior atmosphere and building biome. Hovering around the building, a few butterfly-shaped drones take readings and maps of the immediate microclimate. They return every few minutes to recharge, and their combined real-time data works to maintain the butterfly health.

The building is intended to serve as an object lesson in enhancing the urban environment (including plant life and other creatures) with green technologies, in designing for other species, and in conveying images of new possibilities for the urban environment. This project alone will not save the Monarch, but it will crucially raise awareness about our much-loved insect residents.

Butterfly-shaped drones that take readings and maps of the immediate microclimate.
Courtesy of Mitchell Joachim.

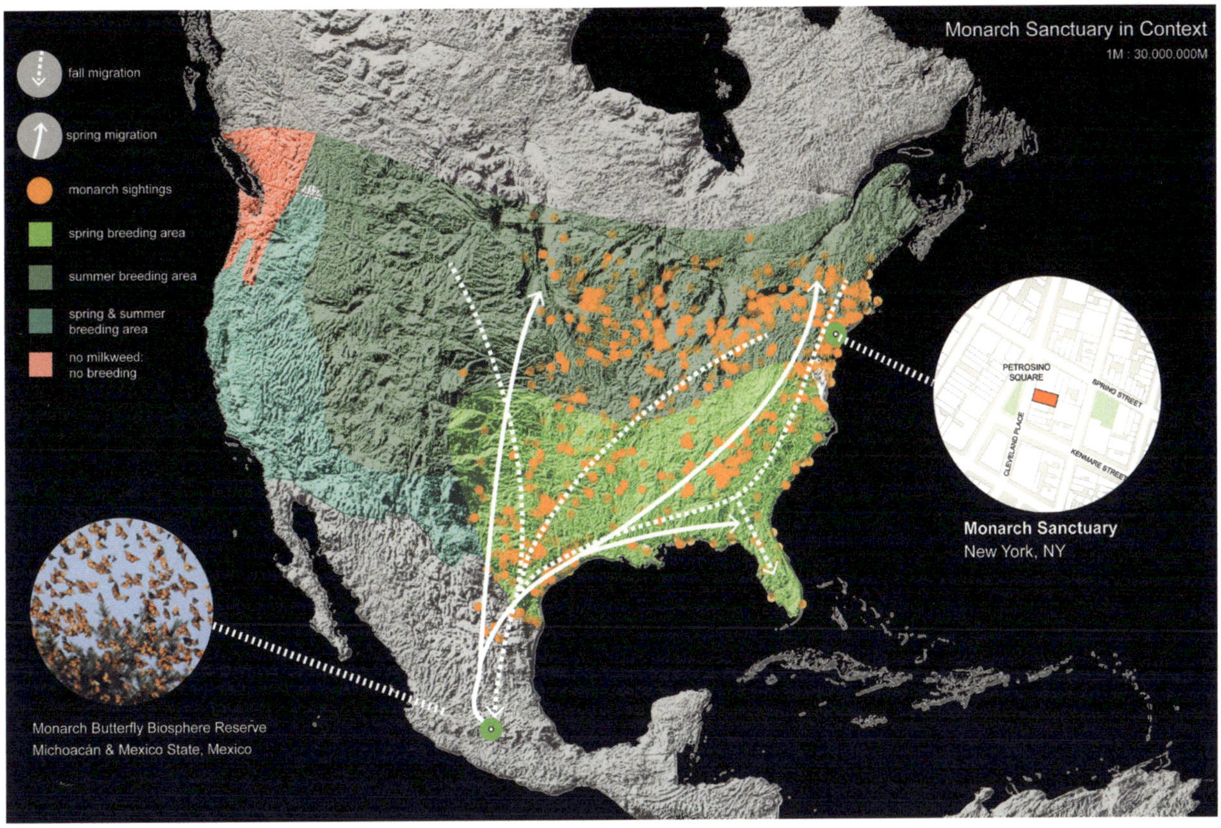
Monarch Sanctuary in Context
1M : 30.000.000M
fall migration
spring migration
monarch sightings
spring breeding area
summer breeding area
spring & summer breeding area
no milkweed: no breeding
PETROSINO SQUARE
SPRING STREET
CLEVELAND PLACE
KENMARE STREET
Monarch Sanctuary
New York, NY
Monarch Butterfly Biosphere Reserve
Michoacán & Mexico State, Mexico

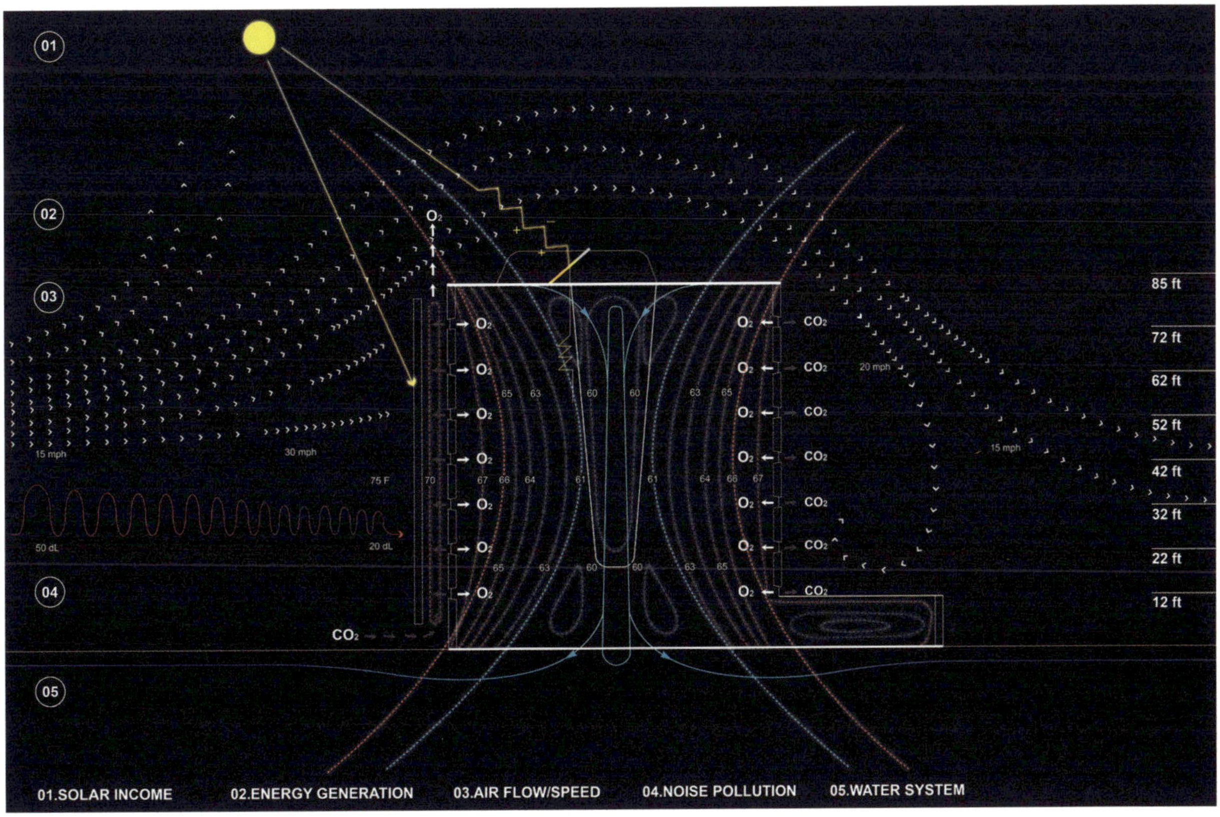
01
02
03
04
05
85 ft
72 ft
62 ft
52 ft
42 ft
32 ft
22 ft
12 ft
15 mph
30 mph
20 mph
75 F
50 dL
20 dL
01.SOLAR INCOME
02.ENERGY GENERATION
03.AIR FLOW/SPEED
04.NOISE POLLUTION
05.WATER SYSTEM

Robotic Habitats

Noumena

Deep learning has paved the way for machines to expand beyond narrow capabilities to soon achieve human-level performance in intellectual tasks. However, as A.I. establishes its place among humans, society will need to develop a framework for both to thrive. A new form of artificial life will emerge, finding space at the peripheries of humanity in order to not compete for human-dominated resources.

A.I. will attempt to improve its operating surroundings to not just survive but be self-sustaining, forming the basis of a civilization constrained at the intersection of nature and technology.

These emerging robotic organisms will begin to manipulate their environment, process resources and shape new habitats through a symbiotic association among the elements in them. This evolving society will trigger the need for robots to evolve into different species, each performing specific tasks.

Project developed for the 4th Tallinn Architecture Biennale TAB Bio_Tallinn 2017. Project team, in collaboration with EcoLogicStudio:
Concept - Aldo Sollazzo, Stuart Maggs;
Design - Aldo Sollazzo, Eugenio Bettucchi, Marco Sanalitro;
Digital Fabrication - Aldo Sollazzo, Eugenio Bettucchi, Marco Sanalitro, Gianluca Pugliese [Wasp], Pavel Aguilar, Laura Civetti, Federica Ciccone, Laura Ruggeri;
Programming - Angel Muñoz;
Hardware Development - Angel Muñoz, Cristian Rizzuti; Interaction Design - Cristian Rizzuti;
Mycelium Research - Adrien Rigobello, Jessica Diaz, Laura Civetti.

Previous page:
Multiple robots establishing novel symbiotic associations within their surrounding, finally conceiving a natural landscape robotically manipulated. Photo credit: TonuTunnel.com.

Drones will explore the environment, searching for resources to manipulate, while sending inputs and instructions to direct ground-based activities. Infrastructures will be built to guarantee life and continuity, feeding evolving generations, processing nutrients and bacteria. There will be a new robotic habitat, shaped by autonomous species driven by hidden, inaccessible forces.

Following page:
Multiple robots establishing novel symbiotic associations within their surrounding, finally conceiving a natural landscape robotically manipulated.
Photo credit: TonuTunnel.com.

Robotic Habitats aims to question the evolution of artificial intelligence into a new species, operating at the intersection of nature and technology in the Paljassaare Peninsula. The installation envisions the rise of a new independent civilization through the extraction and processing of natural resources. The exhibit showcases multiple robots establishing novel symbiotic associations within their surroundings, finally conceiving a natural landscape that is robotically manipulated. The goal of this exhibit is provoking a discussion around the role of AI in our society and the rise of a new equilibrium among the forces ruling our world's ecosystem.

The Noumena framework developed to build this narrative is based on the cross-disciplinary intersection of computational design, mechanical and electronic design, rapid prototyping interaction and mapping. Today, computing tools and rapid prototyping machines allow for quick practical feedback on design solutions and for iteration, experimenting with different possibilities while giving us the chance to select and customize functional parts. Ecology is one of the topics that drives design decisions: our proposed robots seek nature as their main inspiration; design decisions try to adapt and integrate form and function. Technical requirements were embedded into the design process, which mostly expresses itself in the carapace skin that works as a multifunctional layer: it protects the electronics inside and, from the outside, it serves as the substrate for bacterial growth, guiding their proliferation through nervatures that characterize the surface displacement.

The robots skins are assembled with multiple 3D-printed shells, which are connected to the robots' main frame, where all electronics and motors are installed. The main board is Arduino, which controlls the two DC motors that move the crawlers. Each instruction for the movement is transmitted through a Kinect motion sensor input device. The red light placed on the robots is read by the Kinect and sent back to a processing script, which, through computer vision, detects the actual position of the rover and communicates future instructions back to it. All projections are produced in Max msp, animating a transforming landscape, which is built over the different columns hosting the new generation of robots.

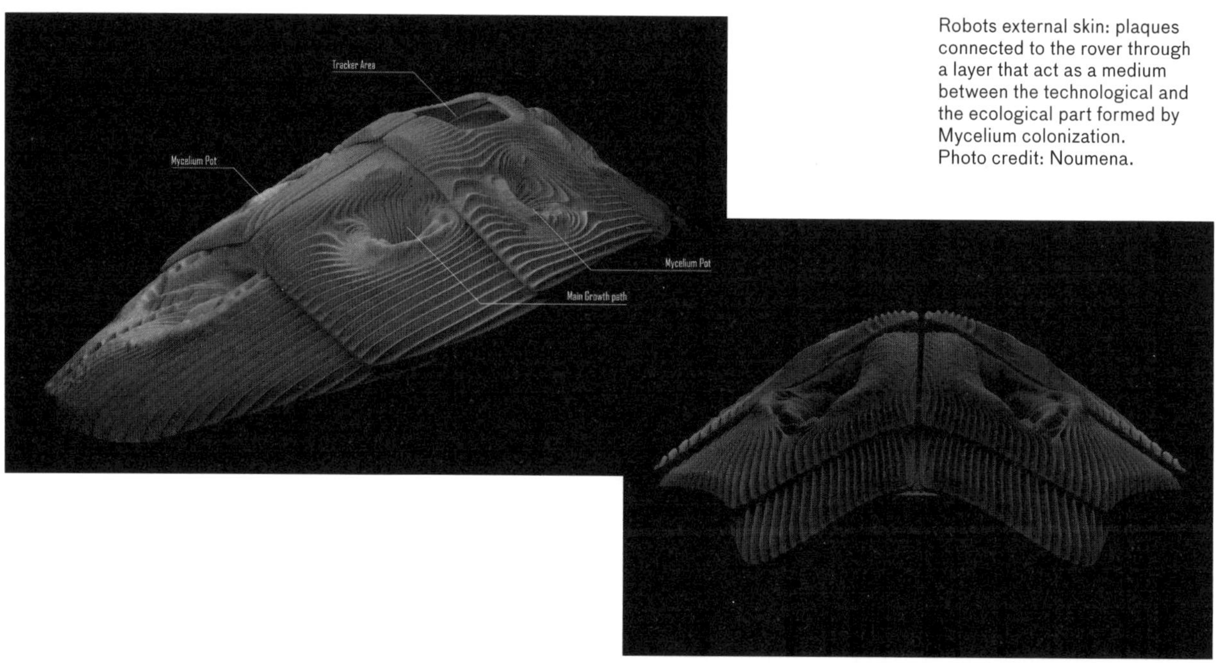

Robots external skin: plaques connected to the rover through a layer that act as a medium between the technological and the ecological part formed by Mycelium colonization.
Photo credit: Noumena.

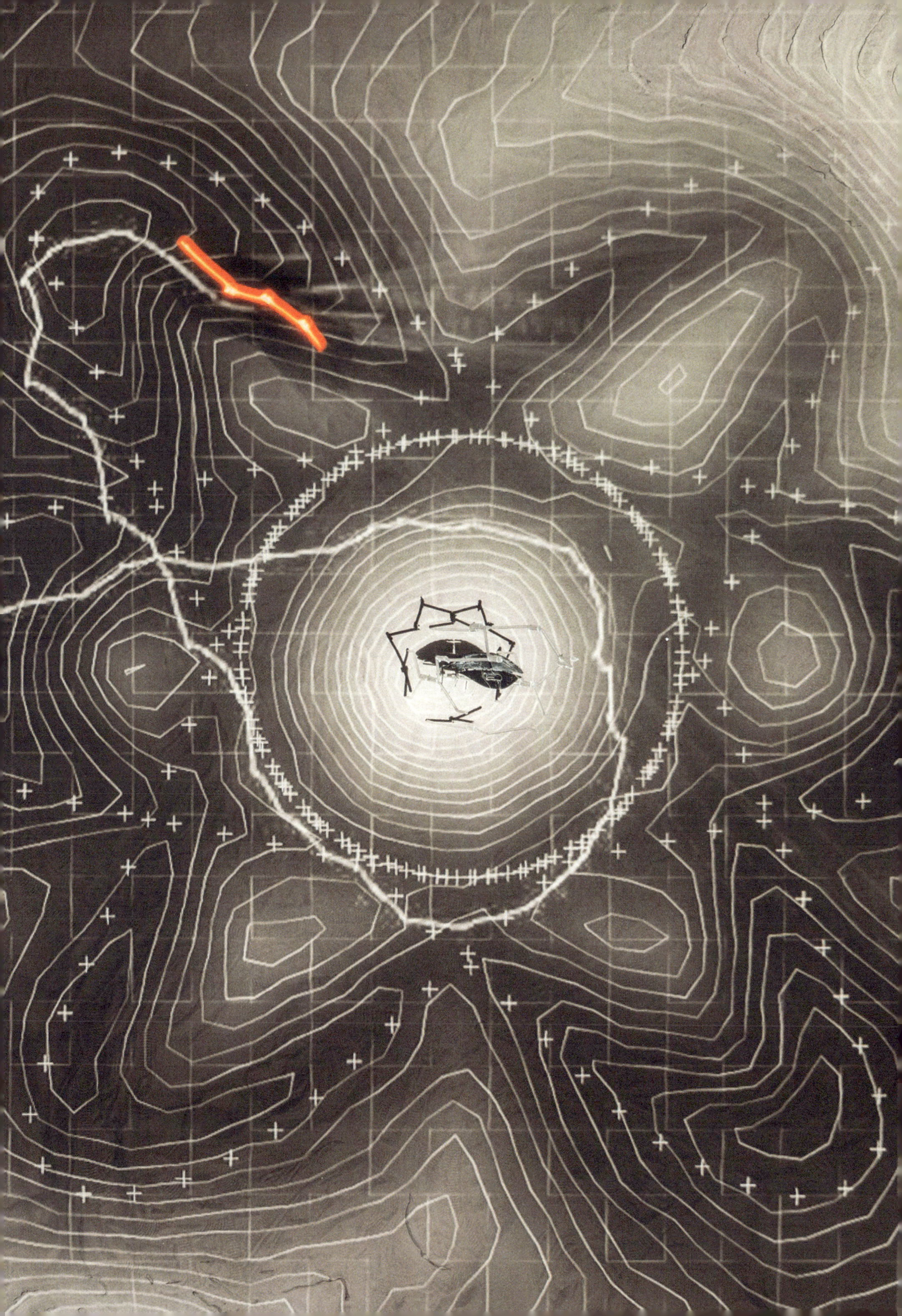

Bio-integrated Design

Marcos Cruz interviewed by Jordi Vivaldi

Jordi Vivaldi Since the end of the 20th century, we have been experiencing a shift in relation to our understanding of the notion of nature: we are moving from a conception of nature understood as Mother Nature (that is to say, a harmonic, perfect and secularized garden of Eden that only humans can disrupt), to another understanding of nature as being highly manipulable through technology (like in the recent cases of artificial DNA or the unfolding of the human genome). How do you think the notion of ecology should be interpreted given this new understanding of nature?

Alga(e)zebo Inhabitable folly for the London Olympics, Euston Square Gardens, London 2012. Detail of the integrated biophotoreactor and of the perforated double steel curvature) Team: mam-arch London (marcosandmarjan); Engineering: Bollinger and Grohmann; Manufacturing: CSI; Biophotoreactor: Richard Beckett with UCL Algae. Photo Credits: Virgilio Ferreira, BREAD.

Previous page: Algae[crete] | A Tectonic Hylozoism. Project of IaaC, developed at Master in Advanced Architecture 02 in 2017/18. Student: Fabio Rivera; Faculty: Marcos Cruz.

Marcos Cruz I completely agree with you on the fact that the separation of what is artificially produced and what has been naturally grown, or has naturally emerged, is almost impossible to differentiate today; it should be read as a continuum. The reason is that, from a micro-scale to a macro-scale, there has been an input of humans; so, the notion of influence and manipulation of our natural environment is so huge that there are very few spots that you could still consider "wild".

The other day I was in a small horticultural park in London. The person who runs it was telling me that it's all wildlife, but they know that it's much more difficult to keep the wildlife as it is than to produce an artificially wild one. They are trying to have only autochthonous plants and keep everything in a pseudo-natural state, which is a tremendous effort for them because there are too many invasive plants and species. This kind of untouched notion of nature doesn't really exist anymore, so they are fighting for something that is nearly lost. We are shifting from a "super-natural" to a "supra-natural" world.

I think there are many levels of interpretation of this phenomenon. On the one hand, it is crucial to understand how we relate to the notion of an artificial, manipulated and mutated nature and environment, and how we can "defend" ourselves against what we have changed. That's actually what you are seeing with climate change and similar profound changes that are occurring on a huge scale: they are partly caused by us, but at the same time totally unpredictable. We don't know how to position ourselves when we're confronted with it.

I am thinking for example about the hurricane season that we witnessed in the summer of 2017, which was clearly the result of how we have been messing around with the environment and provoking ever more extreme climatic conditions, which are affecting us.

But then we still continue building, like on the Caribbean islands, as though nothing has happened.
That's completely absurd. We're in a position where we have to rethink the strategies of how to design and build in contexts that are of our own production.
On the other hand, I believe that there is a sense of great opportunity, especially when we consider that we could still minimize and even reverse climate change. Today we have radically new technical means to design, produce, and create systems in which we can work with and for nature in totally different ways. I am a true believer that humans can create incredible things. However, there are people who believe, in the field of biomimicry in particular, that nature has a perfect model, which we have to emulate. I don't agree with that. I do think that we need to protect what we still have of our "natural" nature, something that has progressed and evolved throughout millennia, and that in many cases we can use it as a model. But we humans are creating new things that are quite extraordinary. We have huge numbers of inventions that are absolutely fascinating, and which are not a mere replica of nature. So, I think that if we join our creativity and our critical thinking together with the powers of nature, we can achieve some phenomenal results.

JV Taking into account this approach to the relationship between nature and culture, and narrowing down the discussion to architecture, it seems essential to understand the terms for establishing today a productive dialogue between nature and architecture. It is well known that both have a long tradition of encounters and dis-encounters, as we can see in the work of architects like Victor Horta, Wright, Nervi, Frei Otto, and many others. However, given the contemporary approach you just described, which establishes a completely new scenario, how should architecture rethink its relationship to nature?

MC The way I connect this dialogue to history is based on the fact that, in certain epochs, we have looked at nature as our model: in some periods it has acted as a formal reference and in others as a structural reference. When we mimicked ornamentation through natural patterns, there was a cultural dimension that explained it, but that mimicking act was, to a large extent, visual. In the 20th century, however, we looked quite deeply into structural mimesis. We were looking at what was happening in particular biological conditions. Darcy Thompson's book *On Growth and Form* was obviously of great influence for architects and engineers, having defined how we looked at the inherent geometries of nature and how they could be extrapolated onto much larger scales. Then, more recently, we have been looking much more at the environmental intelligence of natural phenomena. But I think the great shift now is that we are able to bio-integrate, rather than only being nature-inspired. Bio-integrated design goes beyond the idea of nature as a model or stimulus. Bio-integration tries to find new technological and material hybridities in a world where "natural-nature" is vanishing. Our influence is so profound that we are facing a "supra-nature". We therefore need to be brave and take the opportunity to

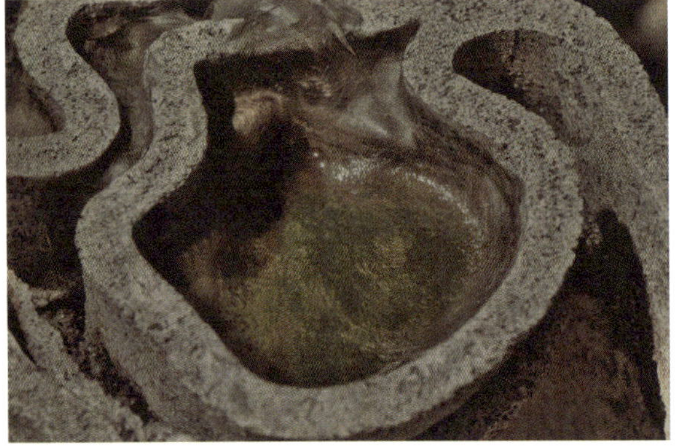

Previous page:
Architectural Biophotovoltaics, 2017. Bioreceptive magnesium phosphate concrete composite with embedded carbon fibre and algae in robotically extruded hydrogel to produce electric current. Team: BiotA Lab / rC7 and Dr Paolo Bombelli with Hoda Eskandar Nia, Eleni Dourampei, Yuan Huang and Zhao Ziwei. Photo Credit: Chris Leung.

Algae-Cellunoi Wall installation with algae growth for Archilab, Orléans 2013. Permanent collection FRAC France. Team: mam-arch London (marcosandmarjan) with Guan Lee and Richard Beckett. Photo Credit: Francois Lauginie.

create new designs that respond to this new synthetic world that we have created. I think that bio-integration goes beyond the extrapolation of natural principles. Of course, we can learn and make use of lots of natural principles, but the main point has to do with properly understanding phenomena like growth, evolution, mutation and material, in order to approach them in completely different ways. We are now experiencing a big shift, in that we are moving from thinking about tectonics, performativity and materiality in buildings to the understanding of architecture as an integrated system of inert and biological matter – a sort of continuous building tissue with a cellular-based structure. However, the notion of bio-integration also emphasizes the fact that nature has vulnerable dimensions that we designers have tried for so long to avoid. Indeed, in this new world order things can go wrong, and this relates to the notion of fragility and unpredictability, which in traditional terms we have associated with rather negative and problematic values, implying a sense of imperfection. I, on the contrary, like to talk about the "aesthetics of impurity", which defines a totally different dimension of design that is biologically infused, and therefore volatile and changing. I find the idea of unpredictability fascinating and full of potential. In this context, we architects need to accept much more the idea that what we are designing and creating are scaffolds for inhabitation, but not only for humans, also for an entire surrounding biota that we depend on in our environment.

JV Taking the notion of aesthetics that you've just mentioned, it is evident that, throughout history, nature has been an infinite source of evocative attributes for many disciplines. However, when we say that we are moving away from a contemplative nature toward a performative nature through extreme technification, it might seem like we are looking at it as a purely instrumental device. How should we preserve or reinterpret this more poetic and aesthetic aspect of nature?

MC We definitely still having this poetic aspect. I am much more a believer in adding new concepts rather than excluding old ones. We are not losing them, we are just adding new interpretations. We understand our context today as a multitude of imperfections and unpredictabilities, which makes us designers work in a distinctive way. I think that is a great challenge because we have traditionally worked for pure and perfect systems, where the performance of materials was completely predictable and finished in itself.
In that sense, the idea of architecture as a "product" irritates me, because the product aims to be a finalized and conceptually hermetic object. I refer to part of my research as "designing for aging systems", because when designs deal with living matter, aging becomes far more fascinating than the preliminary moment of a product in its state of newness. The birth of the product is only a temporarily existing condition that will soon be gone; I like to design for conditions that are gradually changing rather than designing the process of aging itself. If you want to design that, you are being deterministic and trying to say, "This is exactly what is going to happen." I think that's actually one of the great problems we had in the 20th century.

JV This attitude of approaching indeterminacy as an opportunity rather than as a menace seems to be one of the key de-sign strategies of our contemporaneity. Is there any specific instrumental benefit to this, or does it have more to do with a rejection of modernist determinism and an alignment with how reality works according to the latest scientific theories?

MC To be honest, I don't see it from a benefits-based point of view, but from the idea that this is what it is all about: our environmental conditions and what we still call nature are unpredictable. If we are integrating this mutating nature into our design systems, then we have to accept that there is unpredictability, with or without any benefits. Besides that, it's beautiful; from a human perspective, I find imperfections much more beautiful than perfect systems. I feel suspicious of perfection, either because it is excessively controlled or because it simply does not allow for something else to emerge. It's totalitarian.

JV From the moment you situate the notion of benefit as secondary and you introduce the importance of beauty, a question seems inevitable: Do you think that architecture should make a better world or a more interesting one?

MC That's a good question – a really complex one since it touches many things. On the one hand, we are trying to make things better, because we are trying to respond to ongoing problems. I do believe that, as designers, we

Bioreceptive Calcareous Composites, 2016. Multi-Material cast of a magnesium phosphate concrete wall prototype to promote selective growth. Team: BiotA Lab / rC7 with Yuxin Jiang, Xinhe Lin, Zhili Wang, Qungyue Zeng. Photo Credit: Marcos Cruz.

need to be hyper alert to understand how to respond to social, ecological, financial and political challenges and use them as an opportunity to find new creative solutions. I think we need to have enough vision to understand not only what is happening today, but also what will happen in the future. There has to be a functional response to identified problems, and, in that sense, architecture can make things better. On the other hand, as cultural agents, we do need to provoke the status quo, which means that we might "create" problems rather than just attempting to resolve them. The experimental line of architecture has always been a very important one: it puts forward new visions and provocations of what future scenarios might look like. In that sense, we are probably creating more problems than we are solving.
I think that's one of our great strengths: if you think about the utopias that have been conceived of in history, many of those visions got it completely wrong and were rather catastrophic. However, they were a quintessential part of a broader discussion about the types of spaces, environments and cities we really wanted to live in. More conservative roots have always tried to escape from this speculative dimension. I even go further and see the need to embrace the aesthetics of impurity, the aesthetics of what is ugly and unpredictable, as offering the creative power to critique and generate substitutes for our reality. And then there is a poetic dimension; it is probably more related to a sensory and emotional dimension, something that is strongly associated with notions of "beauty".
I personally don't shy away from the idea of beauty. In my studies, I have examined the idea of the "ugly" and the "disgusting" a lot, but what I was aiming at was to find alternative modes of understanding beauty, in a less nostalgic and more radical way, in manners that we feel deeply attracted by.
Again, nature has a very important role to play in this. In very banal terms, if I compare the geometric complexity, fitness and refinement of a biological form with a piece of furniture in the room where we are doing this interview, I realize how sophisticated biological systems are. If I take these shelves from the room and I put them in my garden, I am reminded of how extremely simple the design is, and how we are still in a very embryonic stage of design development.
Plants have developed a complexity and intricacy that is so far beyond what we can achieve now. But, am I trying to mimic the plants? No. Yet, there is an inherent beauty and poetics in nature derived from its sophistication that I find really inspiring.

JV So, would you say that you are working under a biomimetic protocol?

MC No. I think we have to do both. On the one hand, we have a nature-inspired approach and, on the other, we are exploring bio-integrated design. I think they are hugely complementary: they are both parts of the same sphere, but they are just looking at different aspects.
One is more focused on engineering; the other is more focused on design.

JV Referring to this coexistence, we can apply this notion to one of your projects: the "Alga(e)zebo". It represents many of these statements related to bio-integration, performing some natural principles, while at the same time resembling the natural source that was used: a tree. The point is that, actually, as long as it performs as a tree, it could look like any other form. Why is it important to keep not only the operativity but also the image of the original source?

MC The Alga(e)zebo was done without any intention to simulate the visual presence of a tree. Once we were interviewed, and someone said that it looked like bark that was peeling off. I liked that analogy, but I had never thou-ght about it. The only intention of the Alga(e)zebo was to bio-integrate nature on three different scales: on the largest scale, the perforation of the corten steel had a structural reason, while on a metaphoric level we wanted to create a relationship with the foliage of surrounding trees; then, on a medium scale, the gazebo was to be read as a scaffold for plants to grow into the surface lattice; and, finally, there was a much smaller scale based on the integration of algae into vessels where they were choreographed in their growth.
The other intention we had was to display an ornamental and structural form that was expressive: the perforation of the corten steel plate provided a much-needed lightness that held the cantilever in place, creating a patternization that generated the dialogue we wanted with the surrounding trees. We called it an inverted foliage. But the Alga(e)zebo was also a place to be inhabited. I am naturally more interested in the physicality that surrounds space than space itself, or the space that is produced within the physicality of things. This goes back to my PhD, where I explored the idea of inhabited interfaces in architecture.

Previous page:
Dormant Wall //
Computational Workflow.
Project of IaaC, developed at Master in Advanced Architecture 02 in 2017/18.
Student: Evelina Ilina; Faculty: Marcos Cruz; Support: Núria Conde Pueyo, Rodrigo Aguirre.

Bio Scaffold_ The Architecture of Decay. Exhibition of Marcos Cruz Studio in the Master in Advanced Architecture 02 at IaaC in 2014/2015.
Student: Natalie Alima; Faculty: Marcos Cruz. Photo Credit: Filippo Poli.

For me, they were more than walls or columns; they were structures, spaces or environments which could be occupied physically or as a projection of our minds, creating an amalgam or manifold between us and our surroundings. The Alga(e)zebo was something like that: an unfolded inhabitable interface, where people were attracted to sit and project themselves into; a small space of coziness that helped people to regain a sense of orientation within their context.

The Alga(e)zebo was, at the same time, designed for the sake of innovation itself, and that's why I am interested in nature, because it challenges us to move forward.

I am a believer in our "Zeitgeist", which is why I think it is so important to look at what is going on in other disciplines. I like the challenge of each project to push the boundaries of technology and conception.

So, for me, the Alga(e)zebo was a way to discuss how we could build a pavilion with a technology that had never been built before. That was the reason for why we used a double steel curvature system that was perforated, which was initially rather nonsensical.

The company CSI in Germany was very knowledgeable in this field, because they produced many of the Anish Kapoor double steel curvature sculptures. But they had never dealt with a continuous surface that was perforated, which made the material behave very differently compared to its normal state.

The Alga(e)zebo was, in a technological sense, a statement in which we tried to define the ornamentation of steel within double-curvature systems, with both handmade and machine-made plasma cutting techniques. There was a lot of uncertainty during the process of design and manufacturing, but we managed to do it. I love the fact that each project can be used to take a new step. The Alga(e)zebo was an opportunity to answer questions like: "Can we integrate different technological logics when we integrate ornamental features, structural performance, inhabitation, and biophotovoltaics to extract energy from plants to light up the folie?"

In that sense, I always come back to nature and biological systems that bring about new opportunities for design. For example, they suggest new ways to control water retention and absorption, as well as metabolic exchanges that we simply can't deal with in architecture, at least not yet. That is why we have to take advantage of these qualities in nature, while also being inspired by it.

That reminds me that I'm a great admirer of Romanticism: I like the poetic dimension of it and, at the same time, the fascination that we feel when we see something complex that we can't really explain and understand.

But I also love the fact that, philosophically, Romanticism is really seen as part of a cycle of growth and death. Western philosophy has excluded this type of cyclical thinking for a long time, relying for too long on the Cartesian thesis instead.

However, now we are discovering that this circular thinking process positions us in a totally new way; it offers a new perspective to embrace bio-integrated systems.

JV The proximity established between the application of recent technological innovations and the fascination for Romantic aesthethics seems to be one of the main challenges of your work. However, it could be argued that there is a certain nostalgia in that Romanticism, a hidden desire to recover the notion of nature as mystical origin rather than as a performative substance.

MC I don't like nostalgic Romanticism, because I am not at all interested in the "retro" aspects of nostalgia.
I am much more a believer in what resulted from Romanticism. It suggests the idea of constructing and making things differently: the emotional state that we have within the context we produce, thanks to the relationships between high-technology, new innovations and a sense of natural beauty, which I find fascinating.
I consider these aspects conjoint and part of a holistic vision.

JV In fact, your work incorporates research that comes from many disciplines: architecture, biology, ecology, technology. What should the conditions be for a fruitful dialogue among them? What position does architecture take in this interdisciplinary cluster?

MC That's a really difficult issue, because it has multiple answers. The first thing to say is that many of these disciplines do indeed employ very different working methodologies, which are difficult to combine.
The sciences are, by and large, more positivist and linear in their approach, while the arts and humanities are far more discursive and critical. Design is somewhere in between, and contemporary interdisciplinary working procedures are bringing these fields together. This can already be seen everywhere, but it will be even more evident in the future: people of different backgrounds working more and more collaboratively and new hybrid disciplines emerging. I personally find it far more stimulating to exchange thoughts with biologists, engineers, chemists, musicians and so on, than to spend my entire time with architects discussing design. I feel that I can give people from those disciplines something they don't have, and they can give me something new. The possibilities that exist in the "in-betweens" of these fields are far more attractive. I am obviously not the first one to make this argument about innovation being produced in the cross-boundaries of disciplines.
But that really is where the great potential of our current and future design lies. The fact that the boundaries of architecture are growing and becoming increasingly blurred is absolutely wonderful. I like to think of people who use all sorts of design tools – from computational techniques, to robots, laboratory equipment, etc. Designers are hybrid creatures who exist somewhere between these fields in a new breathing ground.
That reminds me of an interesting example: a few years ago, I wrote quite a bit about David Cronenberg's film "eXistenZ" from the late 1990s. When I saw the game-pods in the movie I wondered who was able to conceive these "synthetic neoplasms", as I defined them. Who would be able to design and fabricate these uncanny semi-living objects that were not yet achievable, but at the same time not too far from a possible reality?

Following page:
Design for ageing buildings. Exhibited at the Mexican Consulate in Barcelona. Project of IaaC, developed at Master in Advanced Architecture 02 in 2015-2016. Student: Yessica Mendez; Faculty: Marcos Cruz.

Cronenberg gave some suggestions in the film which were rather provocative: in order to produce the game-pods, there were farms full of organs from genetically mutated amphibians that were used in the assembly of the pods. The main point was that the game-pods implied the existence of some sort of designer-surgeon who was able to create these things – having the surgeon's capacity to control and grow different organisms together, while being able to plan and use design tools to develop the complex morphological, programmatic and aesthetic qualities of the pieces. The game-pods were, for me, the point of departure for questioning what future design could be, which was for sure a hybrid activity: multi-layered and multi-programmatic and totally interdisciplinary. On a side note, there was a remarkable similarity between the pod's design and Le Corbusier's early Objets à la Réaction Poétique, which was really weird and rather intriguing.
But back to your question, architecture is, for me, many things simultaneously. I still believe in architecture's unique power of thinking biologically, tectonically, structurally, spatially, programmatically, all at the same time – which is what ultimately results in making great buildings manifolds and not products.

JV If this feature is something specific to architecture, how can we connect it to interdisciplinarity?

MC To be multi-layered is specific to architecture because conceiving, designing and constructing a building is unbelievably difficult but absolutely amazing, especially in the case of great buildings. The majority of offices, however, produce enormously dull and "flat" buildings. Those who work in a more experimental way end up not involved in the construction of buildings to escape the tremendously difficult and constraining realities of today's construction industry, by focusing on small-scale objects, installations, prototypes.

JV How would you crystallize these reflections in architectural projects?

MC I am trying to develop innovative work with students here at IaaC and also at the Bartlett which fits within a broader discussion about how to situate architecture and design in the future. I am making a big effort with students to step into new territories, because, as I said, I see every project as an opportunity to innovate. At the same time, I think that materializing interesting concepts is challenging, especially when we use design tools. Many students try to use escape tactics to avoid designing, which is why I insist with them to push the boundaries of conventional materiality and form, through hybrid and interdisciplinary methods of design.
The fact that things are physically made is crucial in my opinion. The IaaC, the Bartlett and a few other schools are great places in that sense, because you really fabricate things. What I do with students aims to biologically integrate growth and living systems within the static and inert tectonics of architecture. Then, there is the environment that influences the biological evolution of plants and animals and the buildings we produce. We witness complex exchanges of material, geometric,

biological and environmental conditions, which is why all the work I'm doing has this multilayer dimension that I mentioned before. In any case, the material properties of design are very important for everything that is bio-integrated. I like to argue that today "form follows material", which means that once you understand the material properties you are working with, you are able to design with specific species in very defined contexts.
A few years ago, I defined the concept of "neoplasmatic", which defined conditions of growth outside the body that originally hosted it. But it was quite far-fetched to discuss in architectural terms. In medicine, a neoplasm is a tumor, but from a creative point of view, it is a mutation of a growth system that has its own rules, different from the host where it originally came from.
The neoplasm is something that really has to do with flesh and tissue, as well as growth processes that have a very complex aesthetic. In cultural terms, the "neoplasmatic" introduces a new plasmatic dimension of architecture that is semi-living and that is also bio-integrated.
It also suggests using human and animal flesh as a material for design – which has its own dangers.
For a long time, artists have been fascinated by this.
I liked that, in art and in cultural studies, notions of the grotesque, the abject and the ugly allowed us to develop a different understanding of the body and society.
I knew that in architecture such concepts were avoided, because they challenged the basic aesthetics and technological grounds from which designers departed.
We should not forget that botanic phenomena usually do not disgust us, whereas animal features are able to repulse us much quicker and more intensively.
On a formal level, the "neoplasmatic" had to do with the amorphous, the free-form and all other conditions of geometry that we probably still don't know about yet. For this reason, I parked this term and the research connected with it for a while. I needed something else before coming back to it.
I believe that it will take some time – maybe five or 10 more years. I don't know.

Previous page:
Living Screen // Robotic Fabrication of Algae Based Gels. Project of IaaC, developed at Master in Advanced Architecture 02 in 2014/15. Student: Irina Shaklova; Faculty: Marcos Cruz; Support: Sofoklis Giannakopoulos, Sandra Manso.

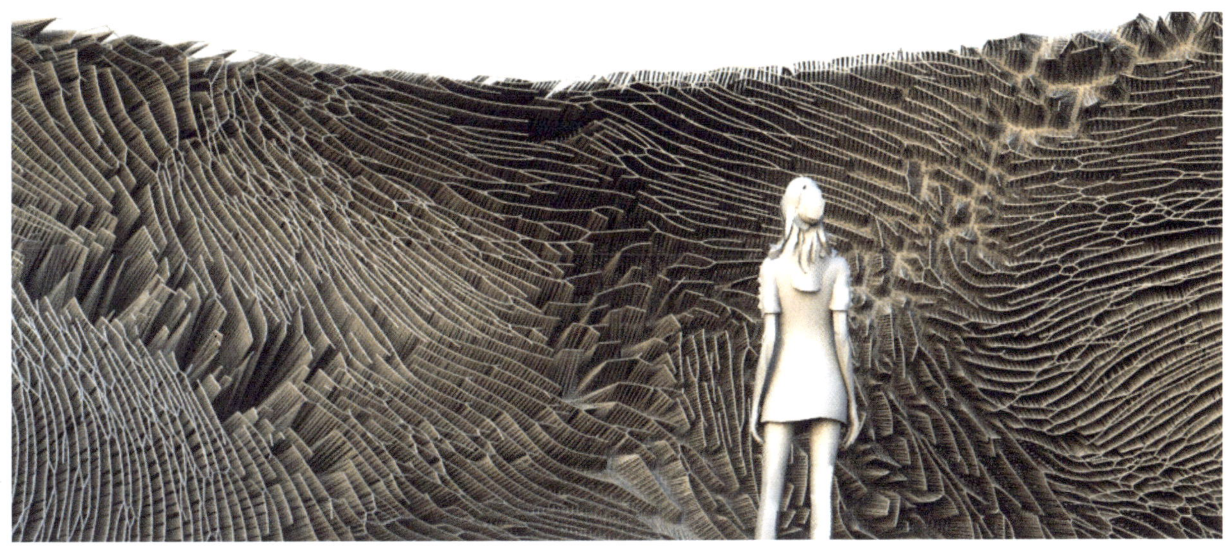

Bottom:
Poikilohydric Wall Highly variable three-dimensional surface morphology to promote a biodiverse poikilohydric biome. Team: BiotA Lab / Marcos Cruz and Javier Ruiz; Computation: Javier Ruiz.

JV So are you planning to move your focus from botanic design to neoplasmatic design?

Top: Hydrogel Scaffolds for Algae Proliferation Robotically extruded hydrogel with embedded algae, Bartlett London 2016. Team: BiotA Lab with Julie Hagopian, Sanika Mohite, Qian Huang, Xinyi Zhou. Photo Credit: Julie Hagopian.

Bottom: Bioreceptive lightweight concrete component with moss growth in exhibition at Super Materials, The Building Centre, London 2016 (components designed and built in 2015). Team: BiotA Lab with Wen Cheng, Sul Ah Lee, Taehyun Lee, Dan Lee. Photo Credit: Christopher Tubbs.

Following page:
Bio-concretion, Project of IaaC developed at Master in Advanced Architecture 02 in 2014-2015. Student: Tobias Grumstrup Lund Ohrstrom; Faculty: Marcos Cruz. Photo Credit: Filippo Poli.

MC: Yes, without excluding the botanic, of course. I think it has an extraordinary amount to offer us, and it is a fantastic ground for experimentation and design. For example, we have many cryptogams around us that are poikilohydric. They are ancient species that are physiologically very simple and therefore unable to defend themselves against desiccation. So, the cellular tissue of these plants becomes dormant when exposed to long periods of drought. But when they receive a bit of water, they immediately switch on and become photosynthetic. This demonstrates that, although small, they are actually very resilient. They are capable of surviving in a wide variety of contexts.
It is really interesting that plants in their evolution found mechanisms to defend themselves against drought, but with the aridity that we are seeing right now, many plants are going to die out in the most xeric environments. The ones that are mostly capable of surviving are the most primitive ones. Poikilohidry is important for me when talking about "bio-receptivity" in buildings: all the external surfaces are in some form or manner bioreceptive, because they will eventually be bio-colonized in time. If we really expanded on this topic and implemented bioreceptivity on a very large scale, we could really shift our cities from being the biggest polluters to becoming active agents in reversing climate change. Rather than collaging green patches everywhere, as you can see in so many fake images, our buildings should become biologically active, or even poikilohydric, to help regularize our environment.
I think that we could respond in a more functional way to the current environmental problems that we have caused. And architecture has a special role to play in this, once it becomes bio-integrated and bio-responsive.
At some point, things will also come back to us, to the human condition. In the art world, it is easier to work with this, while for architecture it is not such an immediate and straightforward theme. I realized that I was risking trivializing and simplifying the concept of the "neoplasmatic". That's why I needed to park it again. But I really think that our future is "neoplasmatic" in what concerns the biologicalization of everything that surrounds us, and with it comes the notion of imperfection, vulnerability and the unpredictability of what we are designing. In this context, advanced software is hel-ping us to predict very complex growing and emerging systems, and it is starting to open the doors to a type of design sophistication that we didn't deal with before. The geometry of biological tissue and cellular structures is more interesting than the geometry of objects as we used to define it.
We are sort of living point clouds rather than surfaces and planes as traditionally understood. This is certainly part of the "neoplasmatic", but we don't reckon what it means exactly yet. We need more time to get there.

15th of November 2017, IaaC
The transcription of this Conversation has been done by the Editorial Team.

LiveCycles

IaaC Advanced Architecture Group

Microplastics in marine environments are becoming smaller and smaller, creating a situation where it is very hard for scientists to properly quantify their impact. The human race dumps a large amount of plastic into the ocean every year, and fauna mistake it for food, attempting to consume and digest it. With the increment of microplastics, bacteria have consequently evolved to degrade plastic segments by breaking them up into even smaller particles. This, however, does not work in our favor, since it only increases the number of microbes and the amount of smaller microplastics, making it more and more complex to quantify or collect microscopic plastic samples. Human beings are feeding the trophic chain with plastics, without having the tools to truly understand the scale of the outcomes.

This project explores an alternative solution to managing the extensive plastic waste present in our marine environments. By investigating methods of aggregating plastic pieces as opposed to breaking them up into smaller pieces, this project proposes a material that gives new life to these valuable plastics.

Project developed for the 4th Tallinn Architecture Biennale TAB Bio_Tallinn 2017 by IaaC AAG - Advanced Architecture Group.
Project team:
Project Coordination, Concept, Design, Development, Fabrication - Maria Kuptsova; Development, Design and Fabrication - Raimund Krenmueller; Computational Design - Rodrigo Aguirre; Concept and Initial Research - Mathilde Marengo; Concept Development - Areti Markopoulou.

Previous page:
The LiveCycles apparatus: a new bio-artificial system interacting with marine ecosystem and proposing a mechanism of plastic extraction, recycling and reuse by the means of nano agent systems.

The studies conducted explored the potential of using bacteria as a method for aggregating the particles, primarily testing Caulobacter bacteria, which forms a bio-glue, and Acetobacter xylinum, which can join plastic particles in a mesh of cellulose.

The experiments shown in the exhibition are the result of a long series of laboratory tests using *Caulobacter*, where the bacteria have been cultivated in agar plates until a very thin layer of bio-glue is formed. A layer of microplastics is then deposited on top of the bac-terial glue, providing a base for another layer of bacteria. This is the start of a layer-by-layer addition process that ultimately forms a material of biologically aggregated microplastics. The bio-glue on the surface acts as an additional binder for the microplastics and improves the overall material properties of the skin. The binding process creates a performative skin that advances over time, therefore providing optimal strength when the bacteria have fully colonized the substrate.

Further tests were conducted using *Acetobacter xylinum* in a liquid medium with microfibers. In this case, the results revealed another method of plastic aggregation by demonstrating that all the fibers were soaked up in the cellulose culture.

The project

Since their invention in 1930, plastics have come to play an increasingly present role in today's manufacturing processes and daily products, becoming what is considered to be an essential raw material. Following the current matter cycles, from extraction to transformation and the inevitable end in waste, there is a growing presence of plastic particles of under 5 mm in length in the world's oceans. According to a new policy brief by Baltic Eye, up to 40 tons of microplastics are released annually into the Baltic Sea catchment, requiring between 450 and 1000 years for these materials to decompose. This generates a new artificial geological layer of marine environment, acting as a precondition for this environment's metabolic development.

The LiveCycles apparatus: a new bio-artificial system interacting with marine ecosystem and proposing a mechanism of plastic extraction, recycling and reuse by the means of nano agent systems.

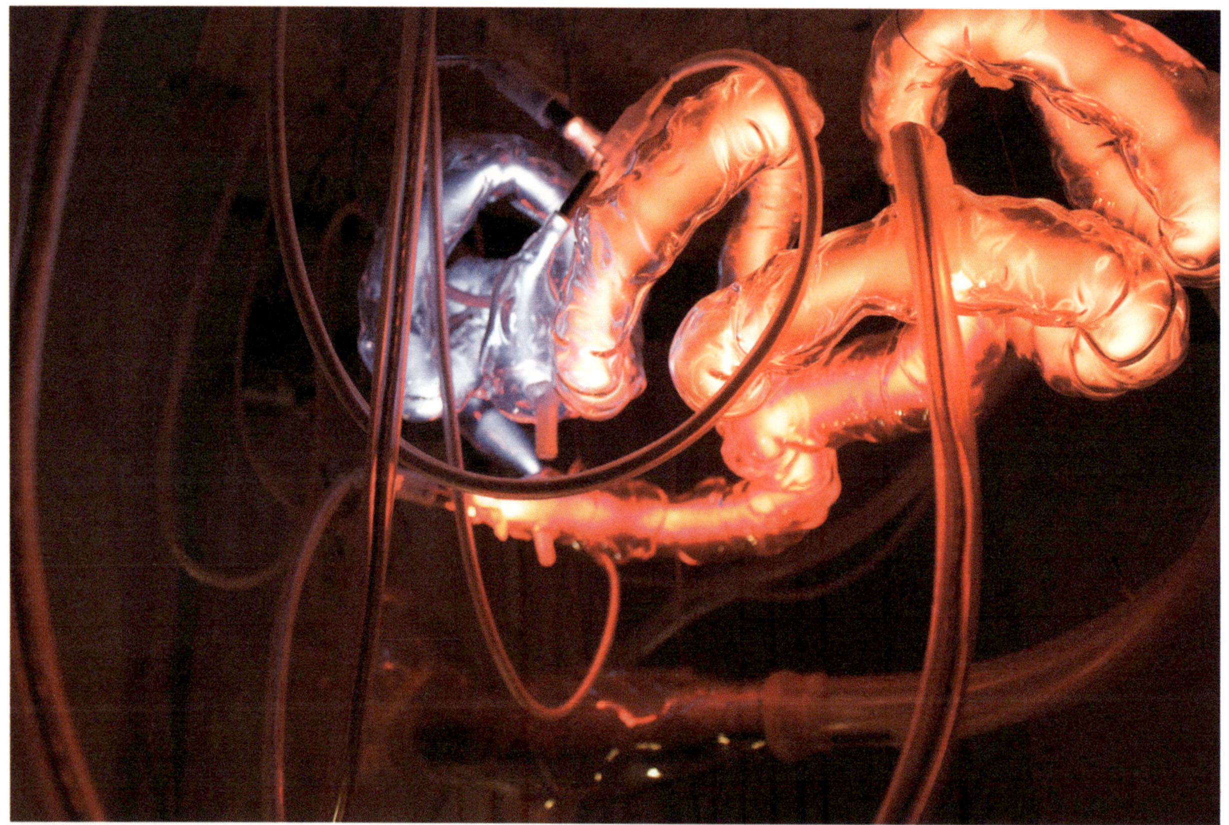

The installation works with Baltic Sea water, firstly extracting the contained microplastics from the marine environment and then, passing through the complex digestion system of nano robot, bio aggregating its particles into a material which can be reused for the further proliferation of this same marine environment.

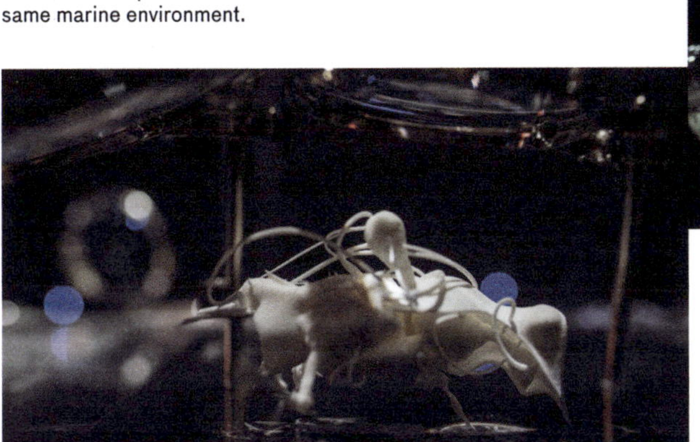

Which emergent mechanisms and systems can interact with this Anthropocene scenario? What new material cycles and processes are emerging? Can we create new interaction protocols and life cycles of matter within this scenario? What is the impact of these processes on the existing ecosystems, ecology and economy of the region? These questions present an opportunity to redefine the marine metabolism, creating new systems of human and non-human interaction with the environment.

LiveCycles is a bio-artificial system which responds to the current challenges, interacting with the marine ecosystem through the definition of possible marine material cycles and proposing a mechanism of plastic extraction, recycling and reuse by means of nano agent systems. The project investigates how small robotic agents might become a new transitional system from built to unbuilt environments, which, in symbiosis with the natural species of the Baltic sea, could act on site, creating interaction between natural and artificial systems. The concept is to engage in a productive matter cycle, fed by the extracted microplastics, towards the generation and printing of a bio-aggregated material through the use of biological binders. The installation works with Baltic Sea water, first extracting the microplastics from the marine environment and then, passing through the complex digestion system of the nano robot, bio aggregating its particles into a material that can be reused for the further proliferation of the marine environment.

By identifying a method of microplastic extraction from the sea water, testing the growth of several bacteria for natural binding, as well as envisioning potential methods of bio-aggregated plastic printing, the project aims to provide alternative material solutions, recycling methods and matter cycles. The installation plays with the scale and invites visitors to observe, become part of, and understand the process of filtration, bio-aggregation and printing of recycled microplastics through the demonstration and simulation of material processes, as well as laying its foundations in already existing innovative technology and research. The installation consists of an enlarged mircoplastic digestion system, allowing the visitors to emerge themselves in the process, fully grasping the comprehensive BioMatter Cycle, from water filtration to the bio-aggregated material system and production.

The LiveCycles apparatus is a new bio-artificial system which aims to change the way we impact the environ-ment and demonstrate how multi-operated processes, from filtering water cycles to recycling material cycles, can also offer live material (bio-material) outputs that can generate new life cycles, becoming a potential for our environment's development and growth.

Following page:
The installation functioning.

T21
T48
T52
T54
T46
T53
T49
R034
C59
R019
R027
R033
R011
T33
T38
T63

Nature as Computing Matter

Andrew Adamatzky

Unconventional computing is not opposed to nature but rather helps us to explore natural forms of computation. In this sense, unconventional computing is not just uncovering mechanisms of information processing in natural systems and using these mechanisms to develop novel architectures of computers; it is also uncovering other ways, similar to alternative states of mind, to compute. There are two strains of unconventional computation. One deals with prototyping computing systems from non-silicon substrates: e.g., physical processes and chemical reactions, plant, crystals, slime molds. The second strain involves dissident thinking, challenging current stereotypes or dogmas, i.e., an "uncommon thinking about computing".

One of the most famous substrates of unconventional computation is slime mold, or *Physarum polycephalum*. It is a large single cell capable of distributed sensing, concurrent information processing, parallel computation and decentralized actuation.

The ease of culturing and experimenting with *Physarum* makes this slime mold an ideal subs-trate for real-world implementations of unconventional sensing and computing devices. Physarum is such a good substrate that we can produce almost anything we want with it: logical gates and circuits, electronic devices (memristors, diodes, transistors, wires and chemical and tactile sensors), computing circuits with functional nanoparticles, and polymers.

Previous page:
Slime mould integrates with conventional hardware. Originally published in Adamatzky, Andrew. "Physarum wires: Self-growing self-repairing smart wires made from slime mould." *Biomedical Engineering Letters* 3, nr. 4 (2013), pp. 232-241. Courtesy of Andrew Adamatzky.

The foraging behavior of slime mold and the way *Physarum* optimizes its network of protoplasmic tubes inspired computer scientists to develop a mathematical model for a non-quantum implementation of Shor's factorization, structural learning and computation of the shortest path tree on dynamic graphs, supply chain network design, p-adic computing and syllogistic reasoning. Slime mold for scientists is like modeling clay for kids: we can shape anything we want from it.

In this scenario, nature is understood as a computing matter, where computing devices are embedded into each other. The brain is a computer, a neuron is a computer, the cytoskeleton of a neuron is a computer, lipid vesicles travelling along cytoskeleton filaments are computers, DNA molecules inside a neuron's nucleus are computers. Man-made computers, as we use them, are part of natural computers, they are just extensions of our inbulding computing abilities, in the same way that spiders outsource their intelligence to their webs. In the future, there will be no computers as we see them now, the human nervous system (and intelligent properties of materials) will be augmented with nanocomputers.

As I mentioned in the past for *Wired* magazine, personal computing will become intra-cellular. Each neuron of a human will be augmented with an artificial self-growing, self-repairing, self-reproducing molecular network. Computers will be inside us. They will grow with us. They will span all living creatures on the planet in a unified computing network. This condition is already making a strong impact on spatial designers: *Physarum* solves spatial problems by developing an optimal network of protoplasmic tubes. We used this feature of the slime mold to imitate road networks and mass migrations, historical developments and future space explorations, evacuation routes from buildings. We successfully used *Physarum* to theorize about migration and technological developments in the Balkans hundreds of years ago, thus establishing a new field of slime-mold-based experimental archaeology. The spatio-temporal behavior of the slime mold has also manifested in musical composition, artistic interacting performances, translating *Physarum*'s responses to environmental stimuli into emotions of an android robot and mechanics of creativity.

In this sense, we live in an unprecedented mix of digital technology and biology, in which the new synthetic ecologies that are created affect the way we live and interact. I believe that the most exciting developments now deal with studies of non-human minds, especially protocognition. Protocognition is the acquisition of information, recognition of stimulatory spaces, building up knowledge, and developing wisdom, sensing, decision mapping, learning, reasoning, believing, being erroneous, showing feeling and emotional states on the part of chemical and physical substrates, and living creatures without a nervous system. I am co-organizing a workshop on protocognition for the Conference on Artificial Life (Tokyo, 2018).

The workshop will address the protocognitive abilities of single molecules and their en-sembles, chemical reactions and media, fluids, patterns and nonlinearities, droplets, polymers, single-cell organisms, including bacteria, protists and molds, and their colonies, fungi, plants, and algae. The speakers will show us how apparently non-intelligent or even non-living substrates behave as though they sensibly and purposefully acquire information about their surroundings, analyze the information concurrently and make decisions based on the analysis. This will affect our life in a way that, in the future, all the materials used to produce the artefacts (including buildings) of our environment will have embedded protocognition: this will allow them to form a matter with distributed affection and intelligence. Humans will be embedded in this matter.

References:

Adamatzky, Andrew. *Physarum Machines*. World Scientific Publishing Co., 2010.

Adamatzky, Andrew ed. *Advances in Physarum machines: Sensing and computing with slime mould*, vol.21. Springer, 2016.

Adamatzky, Andrew. *Atlas of Physarum Computing*. World Scientific Publishing Co., Inc., 2015.

From top to bottom:
Slime mould wire formed under silicon oil. Originally published in Adamatzky, Andrew. "Physarum wires: Self-growing self-repairing smart wires made from <slime mould". *Biomedical Engineering Letters* 3, nr. 4 (2013), pp.232-241. Courtesy of Andrew Adamatzky.

Evolving slime mould chip. Originally published in Adamatzky, Andrew. *The Silence of Slime Mould: Art Words.* Luniver Press, 2014. Courtesy of Andrew Adamatzky.

Slime mould foraging on a 3D template of USA. Courtesy of Andrew Adamatzky.

Slime mould galaxy. Originally published in Adamatzky, Andrew. *The Silence of Slime Mould: Art Words.* Luniver Press, 2014. Courtesy of Andrew Adamatzky.

Emulating slime mould computer on an ensemble of agar discs. Originally published in Admatzky, Andrew, Ed. *Atlas Of Physarum Computing*. World Scientific, 2015. Courtesy of Andrew Adamatzky.

Following page:
Slime mould explore maze. Originally published in Adamatzky, Andrew. "Slime mold solves maze in one pass, assisted by gradient of chemo-attractants." *IEEE transactions on nanobioscience 11*, nr. 2 (2012): pp. 131-134. Courtesy of Andrew Adamatzky.

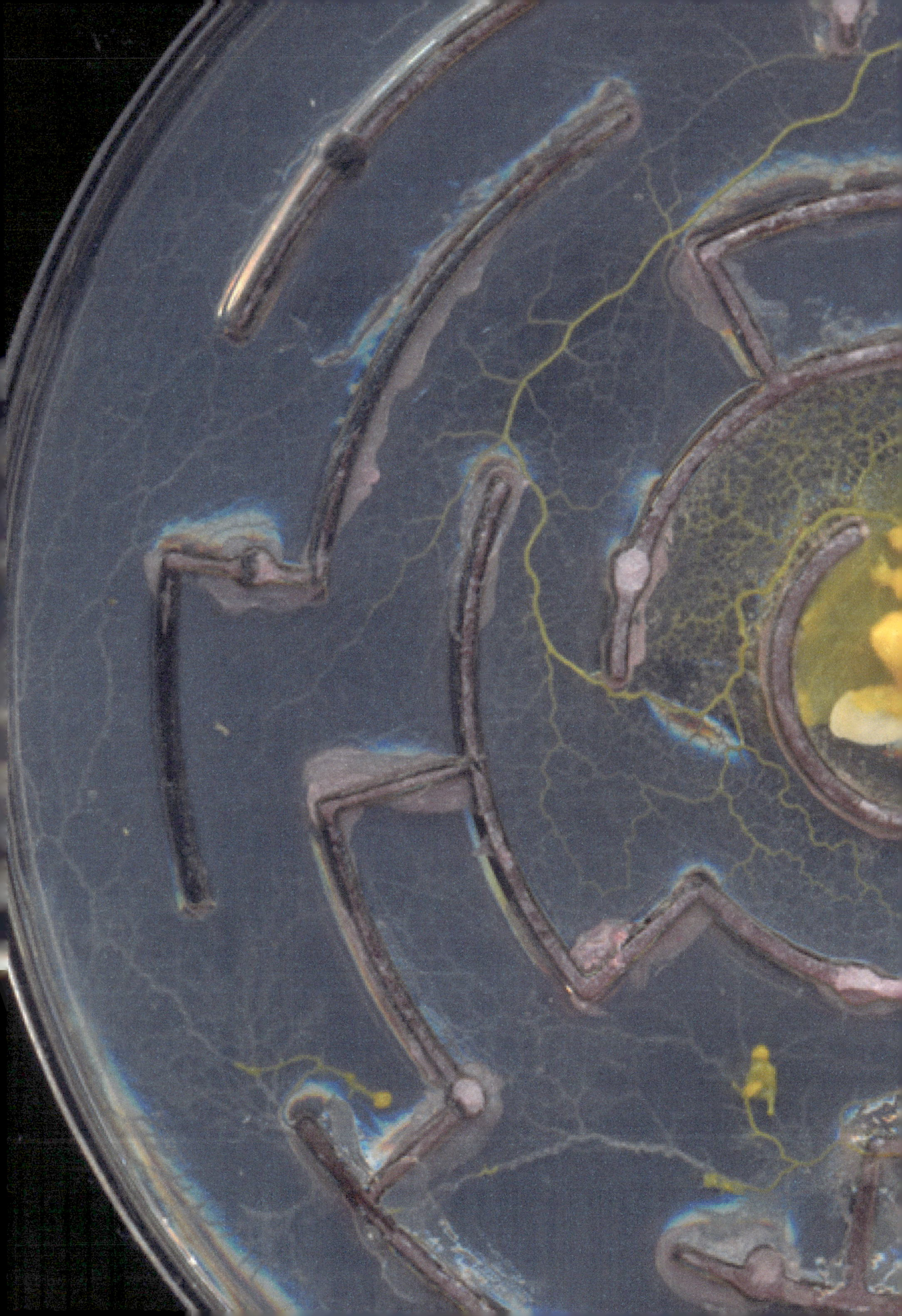

Design Behaviors: Materially Responsive Architecture

Areti Markopoulou

Throughout the past centuries, we have been building in a search for stability. Our - artificial - architecture, made of stone, bricks concrete or metals, has been designed and materialized for stability and durability. These characteristics are those of an age where flows and interactions - metabolic cycles - are related to humans and other living organisms. Consequently, our design strategies have focused on the creation of finalized and static forms; a one-directional design that defines a closed architecture, fully determined prior to its occupancy, and that, more often than not, stands out as a protective rigid layer between the environment and occupants of the architectural form in itself.

Although several futuristic visions towards responsive and animated architecture did emerge already in the early 1900s, such as the work of Antonio Sant'Elia or Villemard, it was the rise of Cybernetics, in the 1940s, that marked a turning point, and provided the technological means, theories and detailed logics that powered futuristic visions of responsive architecture, within a unique cultural and technological context.

Previous page:
Computational Fluid Dynamics (CFD) simulations for wind analysis. Water Driven Breathing Skin: project of IaaC, developed at Master in Advanced Architecture 01 for the Digital Matter Studio 2016/2017. Researchers: Irene Ayala Castro, Montakan Manosong, Ya Chieh Chang, Zina Alkani; Faculty: Areti Markopoulou, Alexandre Dubor, Angelos Chronis.

The emergence cybernetics as a scientific discipline saw new ways of thinking and of interacting with built space, in particular the introduction of questions related to virtuality in architecture, data and feedback, and the unique interactive relationship between humans/living organisms and technology/machines, all notions that could be considered as central predecessors of our current digital age and culture.[1] Flows and interactions, during this period, extend to include tehnology, machines and digital data, rather than only humans and living organisms.

Following the advances in cybernetics and the new thinking in the dynamic relation to object and environment, architects such as Warren Brodey,[2] Andrew Rabeneck,[3] Cedric Price,[4] Takis Zenetos,[5] Nicholas Negroponte[6] Charles Eastman[7] or Yona Friedman[8] amongst others,[9] start to envision, study and draw scenarios where architecture is not static and rigid, but rather flexible, adaptive and responsive to user needs as well as to cultural and environmental conditions.

Furthermore, for the first time in the history of architecture, notions of intelligence and self-awareness are attributed to built space, including the required technological descriptions and means for such embedded intelligence to be implemented.

Although, the architectural behavior and response during the 60s and until late 90s, is mainly achieved through sensors, computers, machines and mechanized systems, initial questions and visions on active and dynamic materials already start to appear in both the architectural and cybernetic world.

Whereas the questions were not explored deeply enough to embrace a new material ecology, the notions and requests for a living and humanizing machine as described by Nicholas Negroponte,[10] or the need of a matter able to actively sense human beings around it and reprogram itself described by Gordon Pask,[11] are the first signs of a responsive architectural thinking that embraces matter as an important aspect of the human-environment-technology dialogue.

The last two decades, advancements on both material and digital technologies saw the rise of a series of built and experimental work that are both based on, and evolve the principle ideas of cybernetics and the visionary responsive architectural scenarios of 60s and 70s. The advances of material science, coupled with computation and digital technologies, and applied to the architectural discipline have brought to life unprecedented possibilities for the design and making of responsive, collectively created and intelligent environments. Over the last two decades, research and applications of novel active materials, together with digital technologies such as Ubiquitous Computing, Human-Computer Interaction, and Artificial Intelligence, have introduced a model of *Materially Responsive Architecture* that places active and dynamic matter at the centre of the design.

Contemporary architects and researchers couple the discourse of their work with notions such as "morphogenesis", "emergence", or "self-organization" in a number of contemporary efforts that seek for a unification of matter, form and function in architectural design and production. Learning by natural morphogenesis, for instance, Achim Menges, professor and the director of the Institute for Computational Design at Stuttgart University, considers that architecture needs to follow an alternative model where formation and materialization are inseparable.[12]

Components of Water-Driven Breathing Skin: **project of IaaC, developed at Master in Advanced Architecture 01 for the Digital Matter Studio 2016/2017. Researchers: Irene Ayala Castro, Montakan Manosong, Ya Chieh Chang, Zina Alkani; Faculty: Areti Markopoulou, Alexandre Dubor, Angelos Chronis.**

Skylar Tibbits, the director of Self Assembly Lab at the MIT argues that the relationship of architects and designers with matter has been always "passive" while matter in its molecular scale is always "active". In contrast to the current model of recombining matter (from top to down) to form geometries and behaviors, he calls for a new model of using properties of the digital world and the natural world applied to the formation of a new dynamic and behavioral synthetic world.

The work of the Self Assembly Lab includes polymers in form of octahedrons that are able to fold and unfold based on humidity levels and create a planar or a 3 dimenssional form. This process is what Tibbits calls "4d printing".[13]

Philip Beesley uses smart or bio materials focusing on the potential of contemporary responsive environments to "care," and on the "expansion of the power of architecture" on its inhabitants, introducing concepts of empathy and emotion[14] while Rachel Armstrong's work, is the most representative of a group of architects and biologists that seek an alive matter through the merge of biological organisms with architecture introducing ideas of "synthetic architecture" , "vibrant architecture " and "soft living architecture".[15] Finally, among others, Manuel Kretzer highlights the possibility of an "alive architecture" and a new softness through the use of "information materials", which are active and smart, and which do not only "carry and visualize information but are also based on information, being artificially created from pure intellect".[16]

Re-Action

Materially Responsive Architecture presents unique possibilities for designing novel performances and behaviors in architectural space. Architectural solutions, for instance, that use expanding hydrogel materials to create dynamic skins that passively cool the interior of a building or public space, bring forward the possibilities of using the morphogenetic capacities of matter to replace motors or actuators creating architectural systems that require little or no energy, to perform in synchronization with the environmental conditions. Hydrogels are polymeric elastic materials with hydrophilic properties that allows them to absorb and retain large amounts of water in their three-dimensional molecular networks until rise of temperature evaporates it producing passive cooling effects.

Such built space systems can be designed, thus, to behave in ways that mimic biological functions like breathe or perspiration, and calls for a focus towards a design process rather than a final form, since this latter varies to adapt to different contexts and stimuli, as in nature, and it cannot be fully predicted. The variation of forms following environmental stimuli, as well as the aesthetic qualities attached to the dynamic formal change, marks a shift towards a more organic, rather than a mechanical paradigm in responsive architecture.

While such material systems can be engineered and designed to behave in certain predicted ways, one could argue that the control of the designer on their behavior and performance is very limited.

This is mainly due to the fact that such smart and engineered materials are being activated to change shape or phase[17] by the environmental external stimuli such as temperature, levels of humidity, or light. Although, environmental conditions may be subject to prediction, they are by no means subject to any control, unless one alters them through artificial means (artificial microclimates).

Co-Action

To respond to the lack of dialogue among users and space performance, we observe the emergence of another family of projects that are characterized by a unique combination of active materials and technological user-based interfaces for human-computer interaction (HCI) and user control.

Aligned with the visions of cybernetics-influenced architects, such as Friedman (*dwelling decided by occupant*), Price (*reconfigured by the users desires*), Brodey (*environment's behavioral changes are affected by the users*) or Eastman (*distributed model of user's participation*), a series of emerging projects explores materially responsive architectural models that additionally to the environmental stimuli, they introduce the parameter of the user desires and needs in their operation. These projects highlight the collaborative and co-creation processes among users and environment that characterize the ultimate outcome of the architectural response.

Examples, for instance, of kinetic structures which joints are produced out of shape memory materials that are activated by the environment but additionally allow users to control and decide its deformation through user-friendly interfaces, present possibilities of an architecture that is not only dynamic and passive, but additionally in dialogue with users who can customize it according to their continuous changing needs. The user-interface and human-computer Interaction technologies used, allow the user to decide on the behavioral change of the structures according to not only his/her needs but as well as according to suggestions that the system can give, based on the current environmental conditions.

Projects of Materially Responsive Architecture that combine both smart materials and HCI technologies present possibilities of empowering the users to actively participate in determining their space performance and its characteristics. Such empowerment, landmark of an experience and participation era that many call for in our digitally-driven societies, has been envisioned and imagined by many architects in the past, but until recently the appropriate technology and tools were not available. Through such projects, the traditional notions of a top down unique design and decision by the architect, is giving space to co-creative processes, in which users might make design decisions as well, and where final form or design is the outcome of a collaborative process among designers, users, material and environmental feedback. The possibility for the users to customize their space and participate in its design and formation, can potentially contribute in augmenting their relation with their physical space, as well as maximizing their familiarization with digitally-driven responsive environments.

Base structure with actuators and wirings of Remembrane, A Shape Changing Adaptive Structure: project of IaaC developed at Master in Advanced Architecture 01 in 2014/2015 for the Digital Matter Studio. Researchers: Ji Won Jun, Matteo Silverio, Josep Alcover Llubia; Faculty: Areti Markopoulou, Alexandre Dubor, Angelos Chronis.

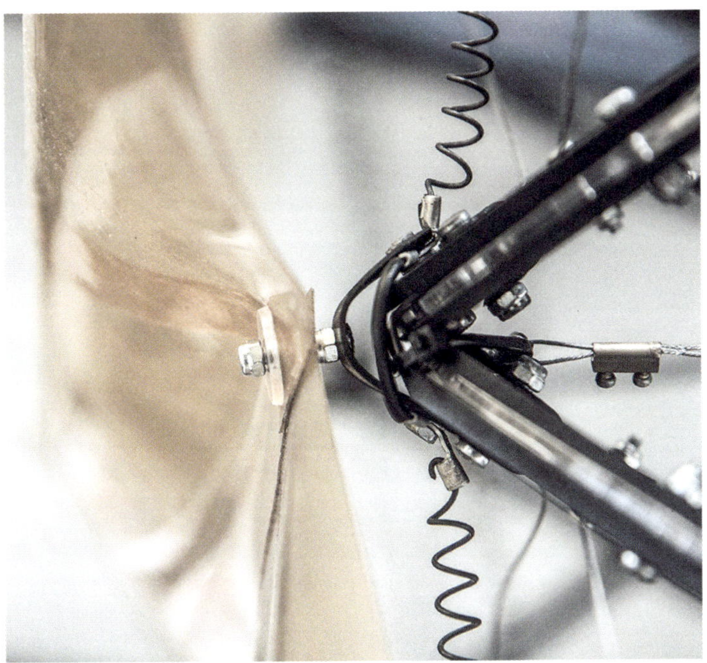

System devices coordination for movement and stabilization. The local stabilization device using Nitinol to release friction of Remembrane, A Shape Changing Adaptive Structure: project of IaaC developed at Master in Advanced Architecture 01 in 2014/2015 **for the Digital Matter Studio.** Researchers: Ji Won Jun, Matteo Silverio, Josep Alcover Llubia; Faculty: Areti Markopoulou, Alexandre Dubor, Angelos Chronis.

The novel merge of functional materials, ubiquitous computing and participatory design calls for a complex design process that is radically different from the one applied when working with static materials, or when working with totally computed responsive systems. Furthermore, the parameter of personalization adds on to the complexity of design processes, since the user becomes part of the design equation, having the possibility to continuously design and change his/her environment.

In such process working with digital and parametric design programs or simulating and programming electronics software is not enough. Rather than choosing among any design variation or any physically embedded computation system, the design choices lay in selecting the appropriate groups of possibilities of all the above that can physically allow the responsive performance of the system in all the aspects of its material, mechanical, and the interaction with the users dimension.

In this sense, design cannot be limited only within the digital or the physical. A cyclical relation among computational design, physical computing and material tests become necessary in the early stages of the design to be able to acquire the appropriate quantitative and qualitative data for processing the design choices. The simultaneous and cyclical design between digital and physical increases the degree of flexibility, variations and affordances that usually reduce in the wake of secure precisions when linearly passing from digital to physical. Wider gradient and variations in shapes, material mixes and final performances become possible when we go beyond the traditional "if this/then that" strict computed equations.

However, one could argue that such systems operate in a top down and linear way, where one input (in this case user's desire) triggers an actuator similarly to the mechanical systems found in the Buildings Automation Systems (BAS) of "smart buildings". They do not operate in a complete feedback loop, where decisions of the user and inputs of the environments are used for the system to learn, evolve and adapt differently every time, as humans evolve and adapt differently while they learn. Such projects present a direct (one to one) relation of user desire controlling the system and change of space. What if the scale, though, requires the feedback of a wider group of distinct users? What kind of systems arise when the scale of operation is not limited in a room or a house but extends to an entire building, a neighborhood or the city?

Self-Action

With the goal of creating a responsive system that operates on a complete feedback model in different scales, a series of Materially Responsive Architecture projects combine functional materials with computational processes of Artificial Intelligence (AI) and Machine Learning (ML).

The term Artificial Intelligence (AI) was coined by John McCarthy in 1955 as the study of machines that exhibit and simulate "cognitive functions"such as "learning" or "problem solving" and intelligent behaviors.[18] McCarthy describes it as the "notion that every aspect of learning or any other feature of intelligence can in principle be so precisely described that a machine can be made to simulate it".[19] Contemporary computer scientists such as Kaplan and Haenlein describe AI as the ability of a system to "correctly interpret external data, to learn from such data, and to use those learnings to achieve specific goals and tasks through flexible adaptation".[20]

The two different modes of operation of the shape changing structure (the first via human-computer interaction and user interface and the second via presence) of Remembrane, A Shape Changing Adaptive Structure: project of IaaC developed at Master in Advanced Architecture 01 in 2014/2015 for the Digital Matter Studio. Researchers: Ji Won Jun, Matteo Silverio, Josep Alcover Llubia; Faculty: Areti Markopoulou, Alexandre Dubor, Angelos Chronis.

A subset of AI can be found in "Machine Learning" (ML) algorithms. Christopher Michael Bishop, a professor of Computer Science and the director of Microsoft Research Cambridge laboratory, describes it as the use of algorithms and statistical models, meaning mathematical models of sample data that is also known as "training data", in order to perform a specific task through predictions or decisions without using explicit instructions or without being explicitly programmed to perform the task.[21]

Applications of AI and ML in architecture promote "Artificial intelligent Architecture" that drives principles from Cognitive Science[22] and this is the reason sometimes it can be also referred to as "cognitive architecture". Cognitive or artificially intelligent architecture is a system capable of performing a range of cognitive tasks including problem solving as well as learning about all aspects of the tasks and its performance.[23] Seeking for Materially Responsive Architecture systems that are able to optimally and intelligently respond to a combination of vast data related with the environment as well as with a wide group of users we find projects that combine functional materials with AI or ML protocols.

Applications for instance of graphene composites to building skins or public space floors allow to create materials applied at building and urban scale that are able to both "sense" and "actuate". That happens because graphene's properties include high conductivity, as well as high capacitive properties.

Being a high capacitor, graphene can become a sensor, offering advantages in all ranges of sensing modalities while being highly electrically and thermally conductive, it can also become an actuator for a system.[24]

In the case of the building skin, graphene nanoplatelets have been used to create a soft membrane skin taking advantage of the capacitive sensor activity of graphene, meaning being used as a sensor that measures conductivity and resistivity (resistance) differences in the material.

The fabricated silicon/graphene membrane is able to identify local deformations, thus, to 'sense' its deformation with high accuracy. This is achieved using an artificial neural network that is trained through a robotic driven actuation process.

More precisely the membrane is being stretched randomly, through a robotic arm that repeats stretching actuations several times. Through the different levels of stretching, it is possible to collect data on the membrane's deformation, as well as on the changes of resistance due to the stretch. This is because different stretching degrees of the membrane provoke varied resistance levels in conductivity.

A similar neural network can be applied to collect other data, for instance, on user behaviors and occupation patterns in the building. Knowing the exact environmental conditions (wind) as well as the user's preferences and behaviors, the building skin, then, could activate different deformations for creating more or less protective areas in terraces, balconies or interior of buildings.

Similarly, applied to urban floors, graphene composites can sense pedestrian flows without the need of any existing systems, such as cameras or facial recognition. While collecting vast data on how pedestrians move in urban space, the system can activate certain actuations, such as for instance dynamic signaling in urban space or the creation of microclimate in areas of high occupation, which in its turn affects the behavior of the pedestrians and their way of moving and occupying the public space.

Such system, becomes a system that operates in complete circular feedback loops where the input (users movement) affects the output (microclimate), as well as the output (microclimate) affects back the input (users movement) that changes again to a different output.

The properties of functional materials (such as the conductive and capacitor properties of graphene) coupled with AI systems contribute to the creation of unique Materially Responsive Architecture systems that present autonomous behavior, meaning the ability to autonomously reason and learn.

Training Single-point Pressure: Robotic Arm used to stretch the membrane on different pressures from where data on resistance changes are gathered and paired with data on deformation in XYZ. Alive - Shape Sensing Membrane: project of IaaC developed at Master in Advanced Architecture 01 in 2017/2018 for the Digital Matter Studio. Researchers: Ardeshir Talaei, Soroush Garivani, Daniil Koshelyuk; Faculty: Areti Markopoulou, David Andrés León, Raimund Krenmüller, Angelos Chronis. In collaboration with IIT (Italian Institute of Technology) and the Smart Materials Group.

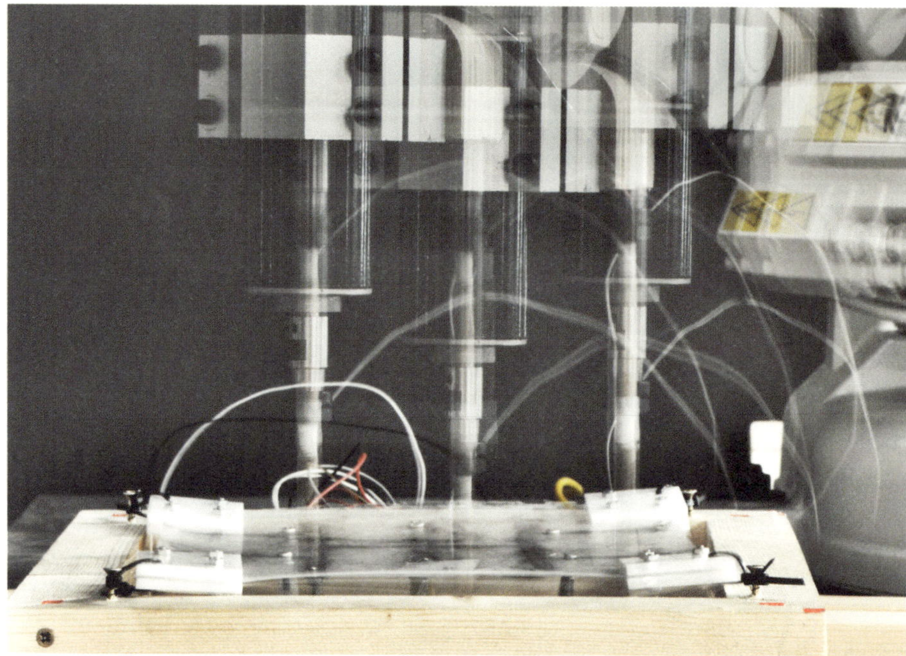

Rather than a space that only reacts to its environment (Re-Action), or a space totally controlled by its users (Co-Action), such systems as the ones described above, reveal possibilities of creating a novel relation among users, space and environment.

In this relationship, space becomes an active agent feeding the behavior of the system with its own input. Changes in the space do not leave unaffected the rest of the agents involved in this new relationship. User's behaviors are affected by the change of physical space, which is also possible to alter their desires.

In the soft membrane case study, for instance, we observe a skin that is able to adjust to wind conditions in order to create protective spaces for users to inhabit. Once this change happens and users inhabit the new space, their new desires or behaviors of how they occupy their house might alter to include a higher level of occupancy or a higher degree of social interactions that can take place in this new protected space. In its turn, a higher degree of social interactions, might mean more people occupying the space which in its turn feeds back the system for a different output (a new shape for instance to accommodate more people).

The new relationship among space and users requires that both agents present certain intelligence, meaning that they are able to learn about their context and develop their own abilities to interact with it. Of course, this is inherent in the human nature, but when applied to space, it radically transforms it into a new agent for dialogue with users that consequently alter the emotions of users towards build space.

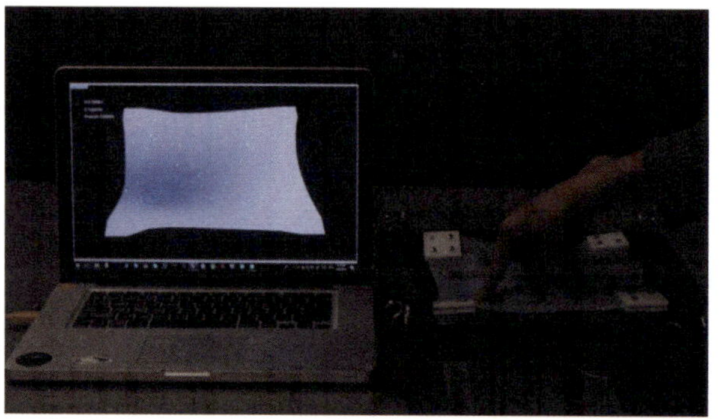

Single Point Pressure Prediction Performance of Alive - Shape Sensing Membrane: project of IaaC developed at Master in Advanced Architecture 01 in 2017/2018 for the Digital Matter Studio. Researchers: Ardeshir Talaei, Soroush Garivani, Daniil Koshelyuk; Faculty: Areti Markopoulou, David Andrés León, Raimund Krenmüller, Angelos Chronis. In collaboration with IIT (Italian Institute of Technology) and the Smart Materials Group.

Conclusions

Beyond the use of mechanical systems, sensors, actuators or wires, often plugged into traditional materials to animate space, *Materially Responsive Architecture* proves that matter itself, can be the agent to achieve monitoring, reaction or adaptation with no need of any additional mechanics, electrical or motorized systems. Materials, therefore, become bits and information uniting with the digital world, while computational processes, such as algorithmic control, circular feedback, input or output, both drive and are driven by the morphogenetic capacities of matter, uniting, therefore, with the material world. Through the applications and implications of *Materially Responsive Architecture* we are crossing a threshold in design where physicality follows and reveals information through time and through dynamic configurations. Design is not limited to a finalised form but rather associated to a performance, where the final formal outcome consists in a series of animated and organic topologies rather than static geometries and structures. This new paradigm, that we could name, as the Design Behaviors paradigm, is characterized by unique exchanges and dialogues between users and the environment, facilitated by all human, material and computational intelligence.

Buildings, objects and spaces are able to reconfigure themselves, in both atomic and macro scale, to support environmental changes and users' needs, behavioral and

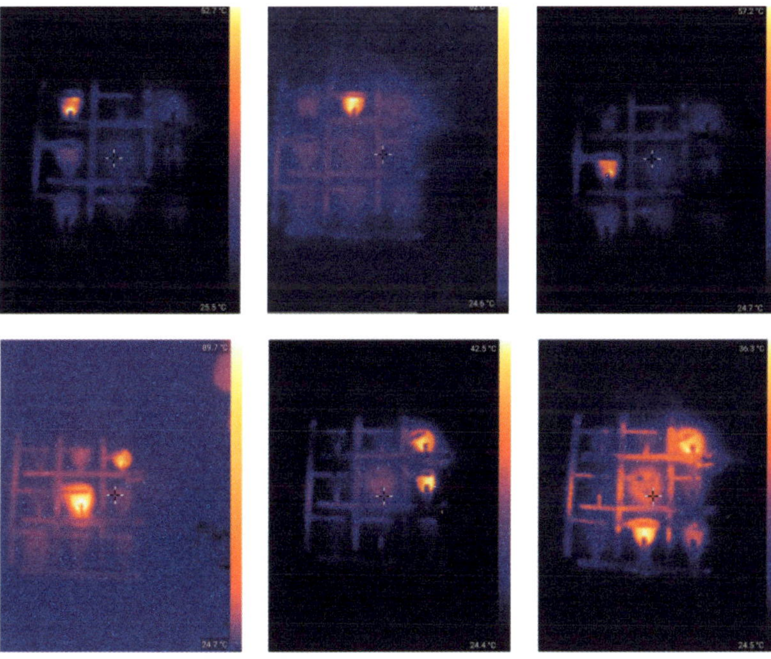

Localized Heating Tests as reaction to footsteps sensing. GNP surface operating as both sensor and actuator.
Synapse: project of IaaC developed at Master in Advanced Architecture 01 in 2017/2018 for the Digital Matter Studio.
Researchers: Nikol Kirova, Hayder Mahdi, Shruti Jalodia, Ewald Jooste; Faculty: Areti Markopoulou, David Andrés León, Raimund Krenmüller, Angelos Chronis.

occupational patterns. At the same time the Design Behaviors paradigm places not only matter and the environment at the center of design and morphogenesis, but also the users, that become active participants of their built environment and play the final creative role. This paradigm shift, boosts new relations between the built space and humans, or among inhabited space and human body and perception.

The new design paradigm is also a new cultural one, in which statics, repetition and Cartesian grids, traditionally related with safety, property and comfort, give way to motion, unpredictability and organic natural principles.

Materially Responsive Architecture consolidates a more direct connection between users and built space, presenting unique possibilities for enhancing the identity of places, strengthening place making and bringing humans closer to what has been traditionally considered as an "artificial" or "non-natural" environment.

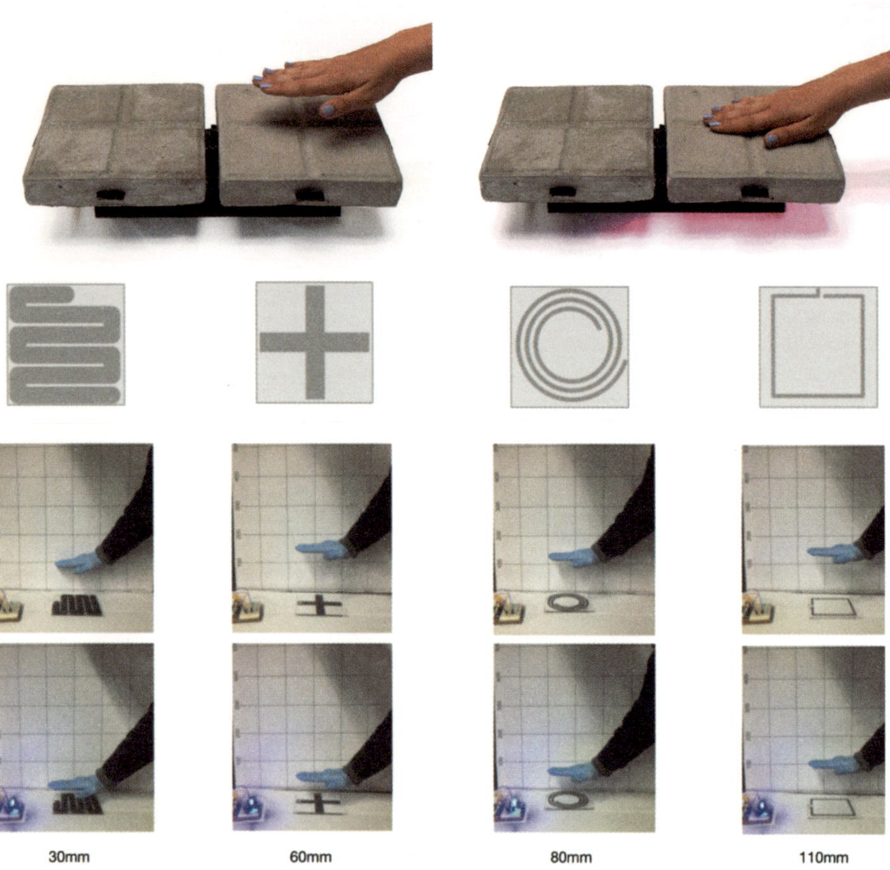

Graphene-concrete composite floor tile, able to sense human presence and actuate by lighting or heating. Different patterns had different sensing range due to their distinctive projected electrical fields.
Synapse: project of IaaC developed at Master in Advanced Architecture 01 in 2017/2018 for the Digital Matter Studio.
Researchers: Nikol Kirova, Hayder Mahdi, Shruti Jalodia, Ewald Jooste; Faculty: Areti Markopoulou, David Andrés León, Raimund Krenmüller, Angelos Chronis.

The new architectural model surrenders its status as a background related model, and enhances our sensory, perception and bodily experience in relation to the inhabited space. It enables a shift in our relationship and connection to it, and we become capable of influencing it actively, co-creating it, personalizing it and eventually being responsible for it. The new architectural environment promoted by the Design Behaviors paradigm becomes an extension of human needs and desires, an extension of the natural surrounding and eventually an extension (expansion) of the human body, while materially mediating between the virtual and the real.

Although, in today's highly digitized and monitored world, many sustain views that the excess of both data and efficient (predicted) decisions might harm the adventurous, playful and emerging character of our cities, enhancing a culture of routine and repetition,[25] *Materially Responsive Architecture* presents a significantly different view.

The fact that it is founded on, and promotes physical rather than purely digital changes and operations, might be a significant way to bring back the crucial aspects of co-formation, co-action, and eventually collective intelligence to the arena of architecture and public space - where social interaction in fact takes place.

While there is no doubt that our future cities will consist in an extensive layer of distributed sensors, actuators and digital interfaces, they will also consist in an additional layer of novel materials, that are dynamic and soft, rather than rigid and hard, able to sense as sensors, actuate as motors, and be programmed as a software. The new materiality of our cities relies on the advances of material science, coupled with the cybernetic and computational power, that can be actuated by the environment to change states (Re-Action), can be controlled by the users to respond (Co-Action), and eventually can be designed and programmed to learn and evolve as living organisms do (Self-Action). The physical space of the city is, thus, the seamless intertwining of digital and material content, becoming an active agent in the dynamic relationship among humans, environment, nature and technology.

Following page:
View of functional shape changing prototype that could be applied in structures or skins.
Remembrane, A Shape Changing Adaptive Structure: project of IaaC developed at Master in Advanced Architecture 01 in 2014/2015 for the Digital Matter Studio.
Researchers: Ji Won Jun, Matteo Silverio, Josep Alcover Llubia; Faculty: Areti Markopoulou, Alexandre Dubor, Angelos Chronis.

References :

1. For more information on cybernetics principles and evolution see: Rosenblueth A., Wiener N., Bigelow J. "Behavior, Purpose and Teleology". In *Philosophy of Science*, vol. 10, nr. 1 (1943) as well as: Wiener, Norbert. *Cybernetics, or the Control and Communication in the Animal and the Machine*. Cambridge: MIT Press (1985, first published in 1948) and: Pask, Gordon. "The Architectural Relevance of Cybernetics". In *Architectural Design*, nr. 6/7. London: John Wiley & Sons Ltd (1969).

2. In 1967, the architect Warren Brodey published a rather revolutionary essay called "Soft Architecture - The Design of Intelligent Environments", where he describes as "intelligent environment", one that goes beyond automation, and that operates in similar logics as self-organizing systems found in living organisms. The environment described by Brodey is highly adaptive, and it is in a continuous interaction with the users that inhabit it. The environment's behavioral changes are affected by the users, but this change also affects back the behavior of the users. Highly affected by the exploration of cybernetics, Brodey claimed that current automation paradigms in physical space were restricting to the "limited human behaviors that the machines can accept as meaningful control", and therefore, we need to consider that machines should become more intelligent by being taught, in the same way as the humans become intelligent. Such steps, could enhance human-environment evolution and he states that "evolution now must include evolving environments which evolve man, so that he in turn can evolve more propitious environments in an ever quickening cycle". For more information see: Brodey, Warren. "The design of intelligent environments: Soft architecture". In *Landscape* vol. 17, nr. 1(1967), pp. 8–12.

3. Andrew Rabeneck in 1969, highlighted the fact that building technologies were "inherently inflexible" and urged for using cybernetics in order to achieve flexibility in architecture. He supported the capacity of cybernetics to "couple automation with predictive technologies". For more information see: Rabeneck, Andrew. "Cybermation: A Useful Dream". In *Architectural Design*, nr. 9 (1969).

4. The most influential architect in responsive architecture, is by no doubt Cedric Price. His "Fun Palace", that started in 1962 is conceived as a "socially interactive machine highly adaptable to the shifting cultural and social conditions of its time and place". Highly reprogrammable, the Fun Palace was able to be reconfigured by the users desires to create leisure, education or event performance. Price thought of the Fun Palace in terms of process, as events in time rather than objects in space, and "embraced indeterminacy as a core design principle". For more information see: Hobart S. M. and Colleges W. S. "The Fun Palace: Cedric Price's experiment in architecture and technology". In *Technoetic Arts: A Journal of Speculative Research*, vol. 3, nr. 2. Bristol: Intellect Ltd (2005).

5. During 1952 and 1962, greek architect and cybernetician Takes Zenetos developed the project of "Electronic Urbanism and the City of the Future". In this project, Zenetos, imagines that the technology is not just embedded into materials and structures but mainly in the human mind, which is able to control and change the environment by signals of communication that require no movement. He was the first to introduce the notion of holistic virtuality and of an immaterial model of architecture and cities. The dynamic aspects and the adaptability of that model are not part of the mechanical infrastructure of the built space, but are driven by and only exist in the human mind and senses. For more info see: Zenetos, Takis. "Town Planning and Electronics". In *Architecture in Greece*, nr. 8 (1974), p. 125.

6. Nicholas Negroponte, the founder of MIT Media Lab and the director of the Architecture Machine group at the MIT has been researching on how cybernetics influence architectural space and how this latter can become dynamic and personalized by the users. Negroponte have introduced the ideas of "computer-aided participatory design", or the "design amplifier", as well as the necessity of introducing artificial intelligence in buildings. For more information see: Negroponte, Nicholas. *The Architecture Machine: Toward a More Human Environment*. Cambridge: The MIT Press (1973) and: Negroponte, Nicholas. *Soft Architecture Machines*. Cambridge: The MIT Press (1976).

7. Charles Eastman has been working and developing a model of a dynamic architecture, which changes are directly manipulated by users. In the "Design Participation" conference of the Design Research Society in 1971 he presented a model that was mainly driven by principles of distributed actuation and decision. In the same conference Yona Friedman and Nicholas Negroponte also presented a model of dynamic and personalized by the users architecture. For more info see: Cross, Nigel. *Design participation: proceedings of the Design Research Society's conference*. London: Academy Editions (1972).

8. Yona Friedman has been one of the most influential architects of the 1960s working on responsive architecture with projects such as the Spatial City, a city with an open interior plan that can be finally decided, formed and continuously modified by users.

9. Other architects and groups of that period working in ideas of dynamic and responsive architecture includes Peter Eisenman, Archigram, Constant Nieuwenhuis, the Situationists or the Metabolists group.

10. Negroponte, Nicholas. "Aspects of living in an architecture machine". In Cross, Nigel (ed.). *Design participation: proceedings of the Design Research Society's conference*. London: Academy Editions (1972).

11. Pask, Gordon. "The Architectural Relevance of Cybernetics". In *Architectural Design*, nr. 6/7. London: John Wiley & Sons Ltd (1969), pp. 494-6.

12. Menges, Achim. "Polymorphism". In Hensel M., Menges A. and Weinstock M. (eds.). "Techniques and Technologies in Morphogenetic Design". In *Architectural Design*, vol. 76, nr. 2 (May 2006), p. 79.

13. Tibbits, Skylar. "4D Printing: Multi-Material Shape Change". In "High Definition: Zero Tolerance in Design and Production". In *Architectural Design*, vol. 84, nr. 1 (January/February 2014) and Tibbits, Skylar. *Active Matter*. Boston: The MIT Press, (2017), pp. 12-17.

14. Beesley P. and Omar K. *Situated Technologies Pamphlets 4: Responsive Architecture, Performing Instruments*. New York: The Architectural League (2009), pp. 16-19.

15. See: Armstrong, Rachel. "How protocells can make "Stuff" much more interesting". In *Architectural Design*, nr. 81 (2011), pp. 68–77; Armstrong, Rachel. Vibrant Architecture, Matter as a CoDesigner of Living Structures, Warsaw, Sciendo, 2015. https://www.degruyter.com/view/product/448453, (accessed July 2018) and Armstrong, Rachel. *Soft Living Architecture, An Alternative View of Bio-informed Practice*. London: Bloomsbury Visual Arts (2018).

16. Kretzer, Manuel. *Information Materials*. Berlin: Springer (2017), p. 16.

17. Phase change materials (PCMs) are substances which absorb or release large amounts of heat when they go through a change in their physical state, i.e. from solid to liquid and vice versa. PCMs are able to reversibly change their shape and/or dimensions in response to one or more stimuli through external influences, the effect of light, temperature, pressure, an electric or magnetic field, or a chemical stimulus. For more information see: Ritter, Axel. "Shape-Changing Smart Materials". In *Smart Materials*. Birkhäuser Basel (2007).

18. Steenson, Molly Wright. *Architectural Intelligence: How Designers and Architects Created the Digital Landscape*. Boston: The MIT Press (2017), pp. 13-17.

19. McCarthy J., Minsky M. et al. *A Proposal for the Dartmouth Summer Research Project on Artificial Intelligence*. Hannover: Dartmouth College (1955). Retrieved by http://jmc.stanford.edu/articles/dartmouth/dartmouth.pdf, (accessed March 2019).

20. Kaplan A. and Haenlein M. "Siri, Siri in my Hand, who's the Fairest in the Land? On the Interpretations, Illustrations and Implications of Artificial Intelligence". In Lin Dan (ed.). *Business Horizons*, vol. 62, nr. 1. Elsevier (January-February 2019), pp. 15-25.

21. Bishop, Christopher M. *Pattern Recognition and Machine Learning, Berlin*. Springer-Verlag (2006).

22. Cognitive Science focuses on the scientific study of the mind and how nervous systems process and transform information.
It is therefore a study that expands on analyzing and understanding intelligence and behaviors.

23. Laird J., Newell A. and Rosenbloom P. "SOAR: An architecture for general intelligence". In Doherty P. and Thiebaux S. (eds.). *Artifical Intelligence*, vol. 33, nr. 1. Elsevier (September 1987), pp. 1-64.

24. Will E. W., Vijayaraghavan A. and Novoselov K. "Graphene Sensors". In *Sensors Journal*, vol. 11, nr. 12. IEEE (December 2011).

25. Rem Koolhaas in his article "The Smart Landscape: Intelligent Architecture" critically discusses that the emerging networked digital technologies affect architecture in a much more profound way than the primary effects of the digital in aesthetics and formal language. These technologies transform the architectural elements from "deaf" and "mute" to intelligent and alive, that are able to "listen", "think", and "talk back", "collecting information and performing accordingly". In relation to expression, he rather believes that the outcome of the fully automated and efficient digitally driven systems, will result in a "sensor culture" with no character, but surrounded by endless repetitions and "routines". For more information see: Koolhaas, Rem. "The Smart Landscape: Intelligent Architecture". In *ArtForum*, vol. 53, nr. 8 (April 2015). Retrieved by https://artforum.com/inprint/id=50735 (accessed April 2019).

Expanding Biodiversity

Eduardo Kac

The presence of biotechnology will increasingly change from agricultural and pharmaceutical practices to a larger role in popular culture, just as the perception of the computer changed historically from an industrial device and military weapon to a communication, entertainment, and education tool. Terms formerly perceived as "technical", such as megabytes and RAM, for example, have entered the vernacular. Likewise, jargon that today may seem out of place in ordinary discourse, such as marker and plasmid, for example, will simply be incorporated into the larger verbal landscape of everyday language. This is made clear by the fact that high school students already routinely create transgenic bacteria in school labs using affordable kits.

The popularization of aspects of technical discourse inevitably brings with it the risk of disseminating a reductive and instrumental ideological view of the world. Without ever relinquishing the right to formal experimentation and subjective inventiveness, art can, and *should*, contribute to the development of alternative views of the world that resist dominant ideologies.

It can subvert contemporary technologies, not to make detached comments on social change, but to enact critical views – to make present in the physical world invented new entities (artwork that includes transgenic organisms) which seek to open a new space for both emotional and intellectual aesthetic experience.For almost two decades a set of research has explored the boundaries between humans, animals, and robots:[1] humans coexisting with other humans and non-human animals through telerobotic bodies; biology and networking no longer co-present but coupled, so as to produce a hybrid of living beings and telematics. Thus, transgenic art can be seen as a natural development of some work where the animate and the technological can no longer be distinguished.

Previous page:
Eduardo Kac, The Eighth Day: Transgenic artwork with biological robot (biobot) of 4 foot diameter plexiglas dome, GFP plants, GFP amoebae, GFP fish, GFP mice, audio, video, Internet. Photo CameraWerks.
Courtesy Eduardo Kac, 2001.

The implications of this ongoing work have particular social ramifications, crossing several disciplines and providing material for further reflection and dialogue.

The introduction of the concept of "bio art", originally in relation to the artwork *Time Capsule* (1997),[2] approached the problem of wet interfaces and human hosting of digital memory through the implantation of a microchip. The work consisted of a microchip implant, seven sepia-toned photographs, a live television broadcast, a webcast, interactive telerobotic webscanning of the implant, a remote database intervention, and additional display elements, including an X-ray of the implant.

The difference between biological agency and biological objecthood is that the first involves an active principle, while the second implies material self-containment.

While "bio art" is applicable to a large gamut of in-vivo works that employ biological media, the possibility to employ a new more focused term – "transgenic art" – helped to describe a new art form based on the use of genetic engineering to create unique living beings.

> Art that manipulates or creates life must be pursued with great care, with acknowledgment of the complex issues it raises and, above all, with a commitment to respect, nurture, and love the life created.

The implications of this ongoing body of work have particular aesthetic and social ramifications, crossing several disciplines and providing material for further reflection and dialogue.

The Eighth Day, a transgenic artwork

The creation of a new mammal, in the transgenic work *The Eighth Day,* allowed for investigating the new ecology of fluorescent creatures that were evolving worldwide. This experience was on display from October 25 to November 2, 2001 at the Institute for Studies in the Arts at Arizona State University, in Tempe.[3]

Although fluorescent creatures are being developed in isolation in laboratories, seen collectively in this work for the first time they form the nucleus of a new and emerging synthetic bioluminescent ecosystem. The piece brings together living transgenic life forms and a biological robot (*biobot*) in an environment enclosed under a clear Plexiglas dome, showing what it would be like if these creatures were in fact to coexist in the world at large.

As the viewer walks into the gallery, she first sees a blue-glowing semi-sphere against a dark background. This semi-sphere is the 4-foot dome, aglow with its internal blue light.

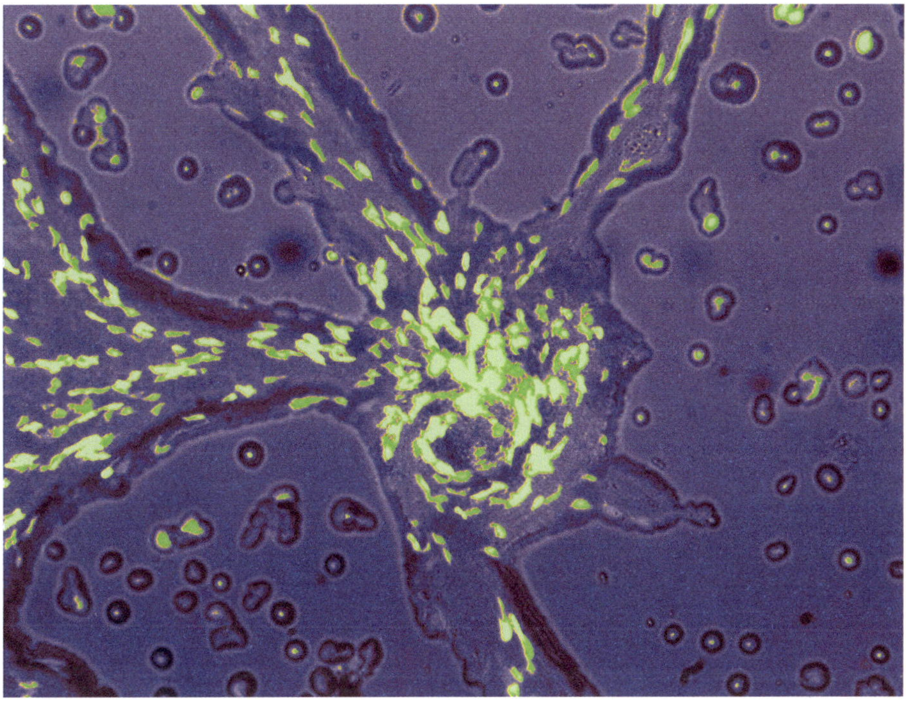

Fluorescent Dictyostelium discoideum amoeba. Courtesy of Richard Firtel, University of California, San Diego.

She also hears the recurring sounds of water washing ashore. This evokes the image of the Earth as seen from space. The water sounds both function as a metaphor for life on Earth (reinforced by the spherical blue image) and resonate with the video of moving water projected on the floor. In order to see *The Eighth Day* the viewer is invited to "walk on water".

In the gallery, visitors are able to see the terrarium with transgenic creatures both from inside and outside the dome. As they stand outside the dome looking in, someone online sees the space from the perspective of the biobot looking out, perceiving the transgenic environment as well as the faces or bodies of local viewers. An online computer in the gallery also gives local visitors an exact sense of what the experience is like remotely on the Internet.

Local viewers may temporarily believe that their gaze is the only human gaze contemplating the organisms in the dome. However, once they navigate the Web interface, they realize that remote viewers can also experience the environment from a bird's eye point of view, looking down through a camera mounted above the dome.

They can pan, tilt, and zoom, seeing humans, mice, plants, fish and the biobot up close. Thus, from the point of view of the online participant, local viewers become part of the ecology of living creatures featured in the work, as if enclosed in a websphere.

The Eighth Day presents an expansion of biodiversity beyond wildtype life forms. As a self-contained artificial ecology, it resonates with the words in the title, which add one day to the period of creation of the world as narrated in the Judeo-Christian scriptures.

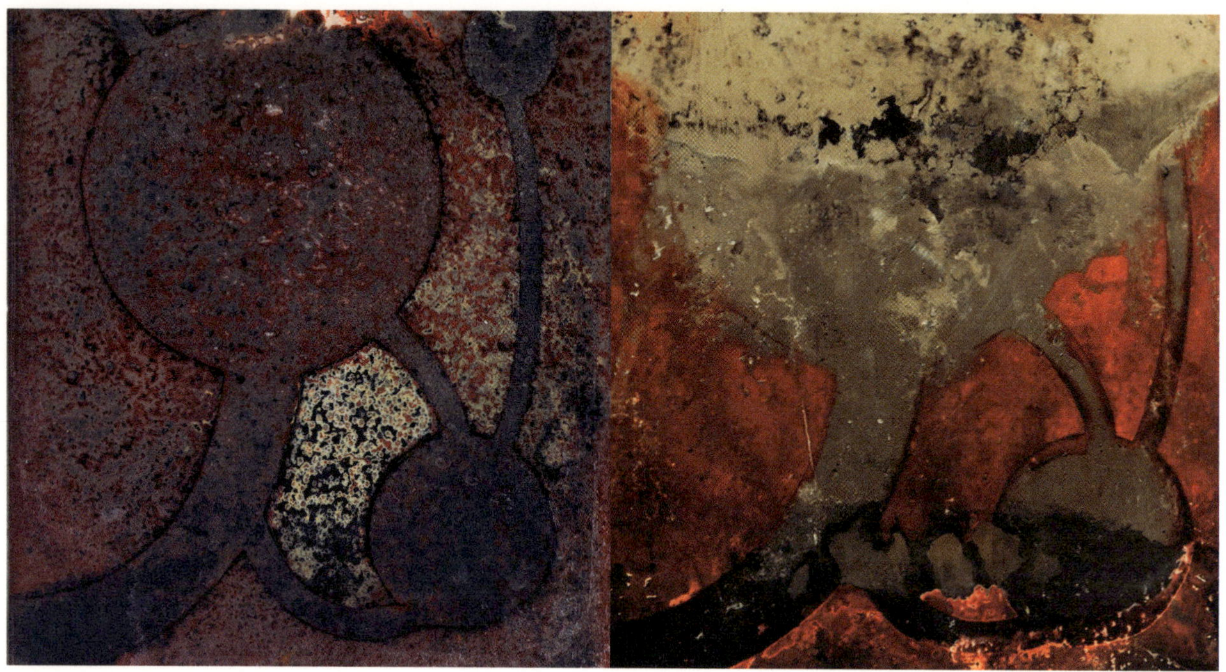

Left:
Eduardo Kac, Apsides, biotope, 19 X 23" (48.2 x 58.4 cm), 2006. Collection Collection Valerio Ferrari, Paris.
Photo: Luke Bartholomew Tan.

Right:
Eduardo Kac, Apsides (2006) Biotope, 19 x 23 inches. Collection Valerio Ferrari, Paris - Exhibition "Eduardo Kac: Life, Light & Language", Enghien-les-Bains Art Center, France (January 21 to April 10, 2011).
Photos: Axel Heise.

All of the transgenic creatures in *The Eighth Day* are created with the same gene I used previously in *GFP Bunny* to create "Alba", a gene that allows all creatures to glow green under harmless blue light.[4] The transgenic creatures in *The Eighth Day* are GFP plants, GFP amoeba, GFP fish, and GFP mice.

Selective breeding and mutation are two key evolutionary forces. *The Eighth Day* literally raises the question of transgenic evolution, since all organisms in the piece are mutations of their respective wildtype species, and all were selected and bred for their GFP mutations.

The Eighth Day also includes a biological robot. A biobot is a robot with an active biological element in its body, which is responsible for aspects of its behavior. The biobot created for *The Eighth Day* has a colony of GFP amoeba called *Dyctiostelium discoideum* as its "brain cells". These "brain cells" form a network within a bioreactor that constitutes the biobot's "brain structure".

When amoebas divide, the biobot exhibits dynamic behavior inside the enclosed environment. Changes in the biobot's amoebal colony (the "brain cells") are monitored by it, and cause it to move about, through the exhibition. The biobot also functions as the avatar of Web participants inside the environment. Independent of the ascent and descent of the biobot, Web participants are able to control its audiovisual system with a pan-tilt actuator. The autonomous motion, which often causes the biobot to lean forward in different directions, provides Web participants with new perspectives of the environment.

The biobot's "amoebal brain" is visible through the transparent bioreactor body. In the gallery, visitors are able to see the terrarium with transgenic creatures from outside and inside the dome, while a computer in the gallery gives local visitors an exact sense of what the experience is like on the Internet.

By enabling participants to experience the environment inside the dome from the point of view of the biobot, *The Eighth Day* creates a context in which participants can reflect on the meaning of a transgenic ecology from a first-person perspective.

Specimen of Secrecy about Marvelous Discoveries

Expanding on ecological and evolutionary issues, the *Specimen of Secrecy about Marvelous Discoveries* is a series of works comprised of so-called "biotopes", that is, living pieces that change during their responses to internal metabolism and environmental conditions, including temperature, relative humidity, airflow, and light levels in the exhibition space.[5] Each of these biotopes is literally a self-sustaining ecology comprised of thousands of very small living beings in a medium of earth, water, and other materials.

Orchestrating the metabolism of this diverse microbial life in order to produce constantly evolving living works (in embracing the mutability of unpredictable circumstances and evolving in response to human care and environmental conditions), these biotopes further develop dialogical principles that can be considered central in this kind of work. The biotopes are a discrete ecology, because within their world the microorganisms interact with and support each other (that is, the activities of one organism enable another to grow, and vice-versa). However, they are not entirely secluded from the outside world: the aerobic organisms within the biotope absorb oxygen from outside (while the anaerobic ones comfortably migrate to regions where air cannot reach).

A complex set of relationships emerges as the work unfolds, bringing together the internal dialogical interactions among the microorganisms in the biotope and the interaction of the biotope as a discrete unit with the external world. The biotope called "nomadic ecology" conforms an ecological system that interacts with its surroundings as it travels around the world. Every time a biotope migrates from one location to another, the very act of transporting it causes an unpredictable redistribution of the microorganisms inside it (due to the constant physical agitation inherent in the course of a trip). Once in place, the biotope self-regulates with internal migrations, metabolic exchanges, and material settling. An extended presence in a single location might yield a different behavior, possibly resulting in regions of settlement and color concentration.

The biotope is affected by several factors, including the very presence of viewers, which can increase the temperature in the room (warm bodies) and release other microorganisms into the air (breathing, sneezing).

Each of these "biotopes" explores a "biological time", which is time manifested throughout the life cycle of a being itself, in vivo (contrary to, say, the frozen time of painting or photography, the montaged time of film or video, or the real time of a telecommunications event).

This open process continuously transforms the image and may, depending on factors such as lighting conditions and exhibition length, result in its effacement – until the cycle begins again.

Eduardo Kac, Natural History of the Enigma, transgenic work, 2003-08.
Edunia, a plantimal with the artist's DNA expressed only in the red veins of the flower.
Photo Rik Sferra.

The biotope's cycle begins with the production of a self-contained body by integrating microorganisms and nutrient-rich media. In the next step, it is important to control the amount of energy the microorganisms receive in order to keep some of them active and others in suspended animation.

This results in what the viewer may momentarily perceive as a still image. However, even if the image seems "still," the work is constantly evolving and is never physically the same. Only time-lapse video can reveal the transformation undergone by a given biotope in the course of its slow change and evolution.

To only think of a biotope in terms of microscopic living beings is extremely limiting. While it is also possible to describe a human being in terms of cells, a person is much more than an agglomerate of cells. A person is a whole, not the sum of parts. We should not confuse our ability to describe a living entity in a given manner (e.g., as an object composed of discrete parts) with the phenomenological consideration of what it is like to be that entity, for that entity. The biotope is a whole. Its presence and overall behavior are that of a new entity that is at once an artwork and a new living being. It is with this bio-ambiguity that it manifests itself.

It is as a whole that the biotope behaves and seeks to satisfy its needs. The biotope asks for light and, occasionally, water. In this sense, it is an artwork that asks for the participation of the viewer in the form of personal care. Like a pet, it will keep company and will produce more colors in response to the care it receives.

Like a plant, it will respond to light. Like a machine, it is programmed to function according to a specific feedback principle (e.g., expose it to more heat and it will grow more). Like an object, it can be boxed and transported. Like an animal with an exoskeleton, it is multicellular, has a fixed bodily structure and is singular. What is the biotope? It is its plural ontological condition that makes it unique.

History of the enigma

The intimacy and personal interaction that characterize our relationship with the biotopes are also present, but they take a different turn in *Natural History of the Enigma*. This series is centered on a plantimal, a new life form I created and named Edunia: a genetically-engineered flower that is a hybrid of human and personal DNA inoculation and a petunia. The Edunia expresses this new hybrid DNA exclusively in its red veins.

Developed between 2003 and 2008, and first exhibited from April 17 to June 21, 2009 at the Weisman Art Museum,[6] in Minneapolis, *Natural History of the Enigma* also encompasses a large-scale public sculpture, a print suite, photographs, and other works.

The new flower is a petunia strain produced through molecular biology. It is not found in nature. The Edunia has red veins on light pink petals and a human gene is expressed in every cell of its red veins.[7] The gene was isolated and sequenced from blood.

The result of this molecular manipulation is a bloom that creates the living image of human blood rushing through the veins of a flower, creating a new kind of self that is partially flower and partially human. *Natural History of the Enigma* uses the redness of blood and the redness of the plant's veins as a marker of our shared heritage in the wider spectrum of life.

The combination of human and plant DNA in a new flower, in a visually dramatic way (a red expression of human DNA in the flower veins), expresses the realization of the contiguity of life between different species. This work seeks to instill in the public a sense of wonder about this most amazing of phenomena we call "life". The general public may have no difficulty in considering how close we truly are to apes and other non-human animals, particularly those with which it is possible to communicate directly, such as cats and dogs. However, the thought that we are also close to other life forms, including flora, will strike most as surprising.

While in the history of art one finds imaginative associations between anthropomorphic and botanical forms (as in the work of Archimboldo, for example), this parallel (between humans and plants) also belongs to the history of philosophy and to contemporary science. Advancing notions first articulated by Descartes, Julien Offray de La Mettrie (1709-1751) proposed in his book *L'Homme Plante* [Man a Plant] (1748) that "the singular analogy between the plant and animal kingdoms has led me to the discovery that the principal parts of men and plants are the same." The preliminary sequencing of the human genome and that of a plant from the mustard family (*Arabidopsis thaliana*, in the journal *Nature*, December 14, 2000) have extended the artist's and the philosopher's analogies beyond their wildest dreams, into the deepest recesses of human and plant cells. Both have revealed homologies between human and plant genetic sequences.

Thus, the key gesture of *Natural History of the Enigma* takes place at the molecular level. It is at once a physical realization (i.e., a new life created by an artist, *tout court*) and a symbolic gesture (i.e., ideas and emotions are evoked by the very existence of the flower).

A sample of the artist's blood was drawn and subsequently a genetic sequence was isolated that is part of his immune system – the system that distinguishes self from non-self, i.e., protects against foreign molecules, disease, invaders, anything that is not him.

To be more precise, he isolated a protein-coding sequence of his DNA from his immunoglobulin (IgG) light chain (variable region).[8] To create a petunia with red veins in which this blood gene is expressed, a chimeric gene was composed of human DNA and a *promoter* to guide the red expression only into the flower's vascular system, not in the petals or the rest of the flower.[9]

Conclusion

The tangible and symbolic coexistence of the human and the transgenic, which has been developed in several of the works discussed above, shows that humans and other species are evolving in new ways. It dramatizes the need to develop new models with which to understand this change and calls for the interrogation of difference, taking into account clones, transgenics, gene-edited beings and chimeras. Although not all of the works discussed in this essay are transgenic, all of this kind of bio art, from "genesis" to "cypher", explores our perceptions of what is "natural" and what is, by opposition, construed as "artificial", "abnormal," or "monstrous".

> The common belief that transgenics are unnatural is incorrect; it is important to understand that the processes of gene editing and moving genes from one species to another is part of wildlife beyond human intervention.

A common example of this is the "agrobacterium",[10] which has the ability to transfer DNA into plant cells through the roots and to integrate that DNA into the plant chromosome.

Even humans have sequences in their genome that have come from viruses and bacteria acquired through a long evolutionary history; we have DNA in our bodies from nonhuman organisms; thus, we are ourselves transgenic.[11] Before deciding that all transgenics are monstrous, humans must look within and come to terms with their own transgenic condition, their own "monstrosity".

Yet this *expanded biodiversity* associated with *bio art*, rather than commenting on what it means to create life, actually creates life.

These works embody the absolute freedom of creation of poetry while simultaneously emerging from the sustained inquiry upon the world brought about through philosophical rigor. They make us question not only who we are as humans but also what that physical identity means in the context of a wide universe of living beings.

Bio art suggests that bucolic and idealized notions of what is "natural" must be challenged and the human role in the evolutionary history of other species (and vice-versa) acknowledged, while at the same time respectfully and humbly marveling at this amazing phenomenon we call "life".

Eduardo Kac, The Eighth Day: Living transgenic life forms, biological robot (biobot) and biobot's eye.

References :

1. See: Kac, Eduardo. *Luz & Letra. Ensaios de arte, literatura e comunicação* [Light & Letter. Essays in art, literature and communication]. Rio de Janeiro: Editora Contra Capa, 2004; Kac, Eduardo. *Telepresence and Bio Art - Networking Humans, Rabbits and Robots.* Ann Arbor: University of Michigan Press, 2005.

2. Decia, Patricia. "Artista põe a vida em risco" and "Bioarte". In *Folha de São Paulo* (October 10, 1997).

3. The exhibition dates: October 25 to November 2, 2001. Exhibition location: Computer Commons Gallery, Arizona State University, Tempe (with the support of the Institute of Studies in the Arts). See: *The Eighth Day: The Transgenic Art of Eduardo Kac*, edited by Britton S. and Collins D. New York: ASU / Distributed by DAP, 2003.

4. In 2008, the scientists who developed GFP into a harmless and useful scientific tool received the Nobel Prize in Chemistry. One of the recipient scientists featured "GFP Bunny" in his Nobel lecture, also published in the 2008 Nobel Prize book. See: Chalfie, Martin. "GFP: Lighting Up Life". In *The Nobel Prizes 2008*. Stockholm: Nobel Foundation (2009), p. 162.

5. "Specimen of Secrecy About Marvelous Discoveries" premiered at the Singapore Biennale (4 September - 12 November 2006).

6. The exhibition was comprised of the actual Edunias, the complete "Edunia Seed Pack" set of six lithographs, and a limited edition of Edunia seed packs with actual Edunia seeds.

7. The gene is an IgG fragment. Immunoglobulin G (IgG) is a kind of protein that function as an antibody. IgG is found in blood and other bodily fluids, and is used by the immune system to identify and neutralize foreign antigens. An antigen is a toxin or other foreign substance that provokes an immune response in the body, such as viruses, bacteria and allergens). In "Natural History of the Enigma", the fusion protein, produced exclusively in the red veins, is a fusion of my IgG fragment with GUS (an enzyme that allowed me to confirm the vascular expression of the gene).

8. Drawing the artist's blood, isolating the IgG and cloning it has been the work of , at the time the artist carried out this work, the CEO of Apptec Laboratory Services, St. Paul, MN. The blood was drawn for "Natural History of the Enigma" on May 13th, 2004 in the premises of Apptec Laboratory Services.

9. The contribution of Professor Neil Olszewski's CoYMV (Commelina Yellow Mottle Virus) Promoter, which drives gene expression exclusively in plant veins was essential. Professor Olszewski is in the Department of Plant Biology at the University of Minnesota, St. Paul, MN. With the assistance of Professor Neil Olszewski, I obtained positive confirmation that my IgG protein was produced only in the edunia veins by detecting the activity of the enzyme GUS (beta glucuronidase), which is fused to the IgG sequence. The detection was achieved through a staining technique. This was further confirmed through PCR.

10. This natural ability has made a genetically engineered version of the agrobacterium a favorite tool of molecular biology. See: Herrera-Estrella, Luis PhD thesis. *Transfer and expression of foreign genes in plants.* Laboratory of Genetics: Gent University, Belgium, 1983; Hooykaas P.J.J. and Shilperoort R.A. "Agrobacterium and plant genetic engineering". In *Plant Molecular Biology*, nr. 19 (1992), pp. 15-38; Zupan J.R. and Zambryski P.C. "Transfer of T-DNA from Agrobacterium to the plant cell". In *Plant Physiology*, nr. 107 (1995), pp. 1041-1047.

11. See Brown, Terence A. *Genomes.* Oxford, UK: Bios Scientific Publishers (1999), p. 138; and Baltimore, David "Our genome unveiled". In *Nature 409*, nr. 15 (February 2001), pp. 814-816. In private email correspondence (28 January 2002), and as a follow up to our previous conversation on the topic, Dr. Jens Reich, Division of Genomic Informatics of the Max Delbruck Center in Berlin-Buch, stated: "The explanation for these massive [viral] inserts into our genome (which, incidentally, looks like a garbage bin anyway) is usually that these elements were acquired into germ cells by retrovirus infection and subsequent dispersion over the genome some 10 to 40 millions ago (as we still were early apes)." The HGP also suggests that humans have hundreds of bacterial genes in the genome. See: "Initial sequencing and analysis of the human genome". In *International Human Genome Sequencing Consortium* v. 409, nr. 6822 (February 15, 2001), p. 860. Of the 223 genes coding for proteins that are also present in bacteria and in vertebrates, 113 cases are believed to be confirmed. See p. 903 of the same issue. In the same correspondence mentioned above, Dr. Reich concluded: "It appears that it is not man, but all vertebrates who are transgenic in the sense that they acquired a gene from a microorganism".

Material Ecology

Neri Oxman

That matter is secondary to shape constitutes the fallacy of design after craft. By nature, and in its rite, the material practice of craft is informed by matter, its method of fabrication, and by the environment (Semper, 1851). As in Nature, when creation *begins* with matter, *morphogenesis*, or the generation of form, is a process engendered by the physical forces of Nature (Thompson, 1942; Thom, 1975). Similarly, in the framework of this essay, *Material* is not considered a subordinate attribute of form, but rather its progenitor. Such is the story of form told from the point of view of matter, and it begins, naturally, with form's predicament.

Form's Predicament: A Brief History

Over the long trajectory of architectural design history, the design and production of artifacts has been characterized by a growing separation between form and matter. In contradistinction to *craft* in which material and form are organically intertwined into a tradition of making, modern design and production have historically evolved away from this integration, or in its absence, towards the compartmentalization of form-making as a process independent of its sources in material knowledge (Sennett, 2008). At least since the Renaissance, with the emergence of architectural theories, form generation has become somewhat of a self-directed and autonomous body of knowledge. Within architecture and industrial design, the most culturally sensitive of the productive design fields, form has grown in both eminence and temporal precedence in the design process to the point that the condition of *form preceding materialization* has become normative and virtually intuitive in contemporary design culture.

With the exception of few pioneering cases in contemporary design, the secularization and debasement of the material realm has become axiomatic. Materiality has become, within the logic of the modernist tradition, an agency secondary to form.

Previous page:
The bitmap printing technique allows for the capturing of material property data in high resolution as a collection of bitmap files printed in 16μ resolution. Curvature informed material distribution (from blue to green). Design: Neri Oxman in collaboration with Prof. W. Craig Carter, Objet Ltd., and The Mathworks, Centre Pompidou, Paris 2012.
Photo credit: Yoram Reshef.

Examples of bitmap printing demonstrating formal variation in color, thickness, porosity. Design: Neri Oxman in collaboration with Prof. Craig Carter, Objet Ltd., and The Mathworks, Centre Pompidou, Paris 2012. Photo credit: Yoram Reshef.

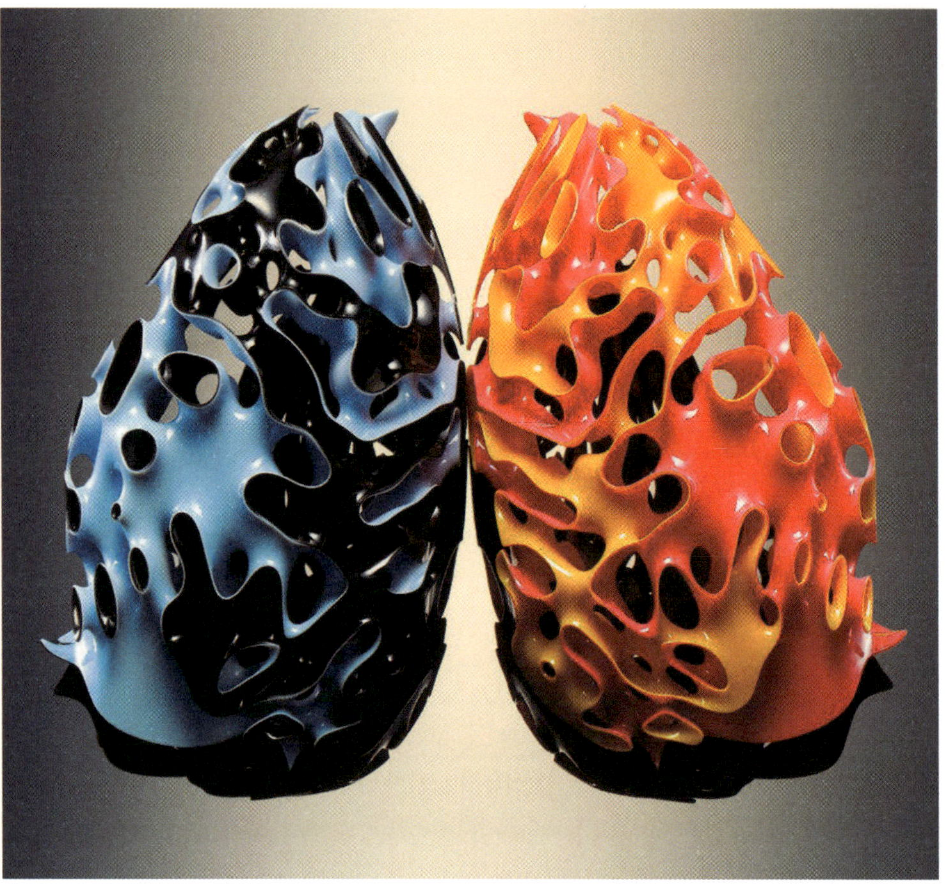

The Industrial Revolution lay open the door to machine-based manufacturing and mass production. The creation of form was now to be conceived and created by the power of industrial automation, detached and independent of environmental forces and influences. The values promoted by ancient crafts (not unlike Nature's way), pronounced by the integration of material substance and construction methods, once within the province of the craftsman, were abandoned while in their place emerged a design practice based on values of mass production. Fast, cheap, repetitive and modular building types and parts were synonymous with Ford's visionary dream. Industry's victory aside, it appeared as if design's propinquity to ancient crafts and its design expressions as portrayed by vernacular forms of design was now doomed lost; and with it the intimate context of material technologies. Eventually, this non-material approach to the design and the automation of construction were to be reinforced under the command of computer aided design and engineering (Jencks, 1984).

The Digital Revolution, which marked the shift from analog to digital technology, has transformed the designer's drafting board into a digital canvas. Form, it seemed, was now divorced completely from the physical reality of its manifestation.

This new design space afforded much liberation in formal expression, but it has also broadened the gap between form and matter, and made the hierarchical and sequential separation of modeling, analysis and fabrication processes infinitely more pronounced.

The implementation and broad absorption of enhanced computational design tools in architectural practice has, since the early nineties, motivated a renaissance of the *formalist project* in architecture; geometrically complex shapes became emblems of creativity in digital design environments and supported the design mastery of complex geometries in form-generation. This formal and geometric design orientation has also addressed "free form" design and architecture along with their enabling technologies as part of the larger design phenomenon of "non-standard" form.

Designing (with) Nature: Towards a New Materiality

Today, perhaps under the imperatives of growing recognition of the ecological failures of modern design, inspired by the growing presence of advanced fabrication methods, design culture is witnessing a *new materiality*. Within the last decade in both industrial design and architecture, a new body of knowledge is emerging within architectural praxis.

Examples of the growing interest in the technological potential of innovative material usage and material innovation as a source of design generation are developments in biomaterials, mediated and responsive materials, as well as composite materials. With the growing relevance of "materialization", new frontiers of material science and digital fabrication are supporting the emergence of new perspectives in architectural and industrial design. Thus the role of digital design research as the enabling environment of the transformation to a new age of material-based design in various design disciplines has become the cutting edge of computational design research. Here we are at the cusp of a new paradigm inspired by the *Troika* structure of craft, at the interaction of Materials Science, Digital Fabrication and the environment.

"Material Ecology is an emerging field in design denoting informed relations between products, buildings, systems, and their environment (2010)."

Defined as the study and design of products and processes integrating environmentally aware computational form-generation and digital fabrication, the field operates at the intersection of Biology, Material Science & Engineering, and Computer Science with emphasis on environmentally informed digital design and fabrication.

Bitmap Printing: a Fabricating Nature

With the advent of digital fabrication techniques and technologies, digital material representations such as voxels (3-D pixels) and maxels (a portmanteau of the words 'material' and 'voxel') have come to represent material ingredients, for instance in the context of additive manufacturing processes. Designers are now able to compute material properties and behavior integrated into form-generation procedures. Motivated by the prospect of designing material behavior, a novel design and technological approach for biologically-inspired layered fabrication entitled *Bitmap Printing* has been defined, implemented and explored by the author, in collaboration with Objet Ltd., The Mathworks and in the context of new design work commissioned by the Centre Pompidou (Paris).

In this collection, 18 prototypes for the human body were fabricated, designed to augment human function such as enhancing strength, promoting flexibility, providing for comfort, or exploring some functional combination. The aim was to implement material property and behavior combinations accommodating for multiple functions in the design of human armors including helmets, corsets, hip splints and various prosthetic devices.

Specifically, the work explored strategies for the integration of protective functions with flexibility and comfort implementing functional gradient digital fabrication (Oxman, 2011, C). These experiments lay the methodological foundations for the generation of heterogeneous and functional prototype development using structural materials for humanoid armor. In order to address geometrical constraints and allow for material organization modulation, both anatomical and physiological mapping were executed during the analysis and the synthesis stages.

Anatomical & Physiological Mappings (Analysis):

Combining global organismal hierarchies informed by anatomical data with local tissue composition mappings informed by physiological data (i.e. μCT scans) the aim was to achieve a fully integrated armor which varies its mechanical, chemical, environmental and thermal properties accommodating geometrical (anatomical) features and physical (physiological) properties (Oxman, 2009).

Anatomical & Physiological Fabrication Strategy (Synthesis):

On global anatomical scale, basic geometrical data describing the anatomical features as transformable meshes were extracted. This network of curves and surfaces guided the distribution of material properties as behavioral patches relating to the skeletal and muscular systems. On the local physiological scale, μCT scan data converted to material distribution data informed the allocation of stiff and soft materials. A novel digital fabrication method entitled *Bitmap Printing* that facilitates the 3d printing of 16μ physical bits was implemented to support high-resolution digital fabrication of heterogeneous functional material gradients. Each material component within the overall armor construction was designed and printed with varying physical properties informed by multi-scalar mappings.

The following example illustrates the Bitmap Printing concept and technique, developed in collaboration with Objet, Ltd., The Mathworks and Uformia for Centre Georges Pompidou (1012).

The final head shield introduces variable thickness of the shell, informed by anatomical and physiological data derived from real human skull μCT scan data. Medical scan data of a human head is selected from an open repository.

Two sets of data are created and trimmed from the scan using medical imagining software simulating the hard tissue (skull) and the soft tissue (skin and muscle) (Fryazinov, 2011). Combined, these two data sets make up the bone-to-skin threshold informing helmet thickness and material composition according to its biological counterpart such that bony perturbations in the skull are shielded with soft lamellas designed as spatial sutures.

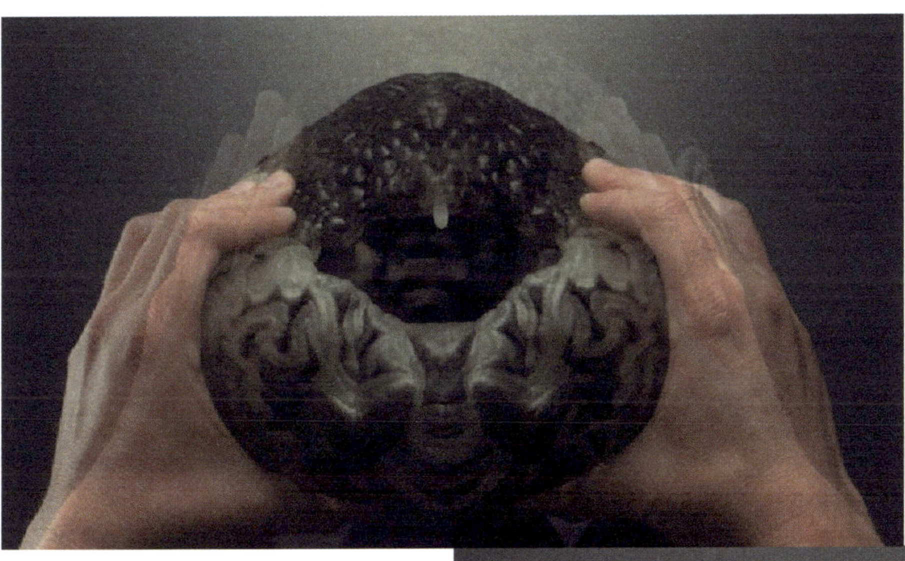

Tissue composition data extracted from μCT scan analysis informs geometrical and physical material properties in the design of a helmet. Design: Neri Oxman in collaboration with Prof. Craig Carter, Objet Ltd., The Mathworks, and Turlif Vilbrandt, Centre Pompidou, Paris 2012. Photo credit: Yoram Reshef.

What Does a Pixel Want to Be?
Towards a Material Ecology

The ability to design, analyze and fabricate using a single material unit implies unity of physical and digital matter, enabling nearly seamless mappings between environmental constraints, fabrication methods and material expression (Oxman, 2010, 2011A, B).

Such unity - like that found in natural bone, a bird's nest, a typical African hut and a woven basket - might promote a truly ecological design paradigm, facilitating formal expression constrained by, and supportive of, its hosting environment.

Like Kahn's brick arch (Kahn, 1969), the units of digital matter may be informed with various functions on their way to become and contribute to larger material organizations.

The designer's voxel is equivalent to Kahn's brick, in that when combined, these material units can self-organize by way of mediating their physical properties with their external environment. Ultimately, the faculty to author new forms of expression will depend on the craft triptych (matter, fabrication, and environment) and its integration into the design practice as an undifferentiated scheme, able to process matter into shape as informed by the environment. Once achieved, architectural design will have arrived at an ecology of the artificial: a *Material Ecology*.

The bitmap printing technique allows for the capturing of material property data in high resolution as a collection of bitmap files printed in 16μ resolution. Curvature informed material distribution (from blue to green). Design: Neri Oxman in collaboration with Prof. W. Craig Carter, Objet Ltd., and The Mathworks, Centre Pompidou, Paris 2012. Photo credit: Yoram Reshef.

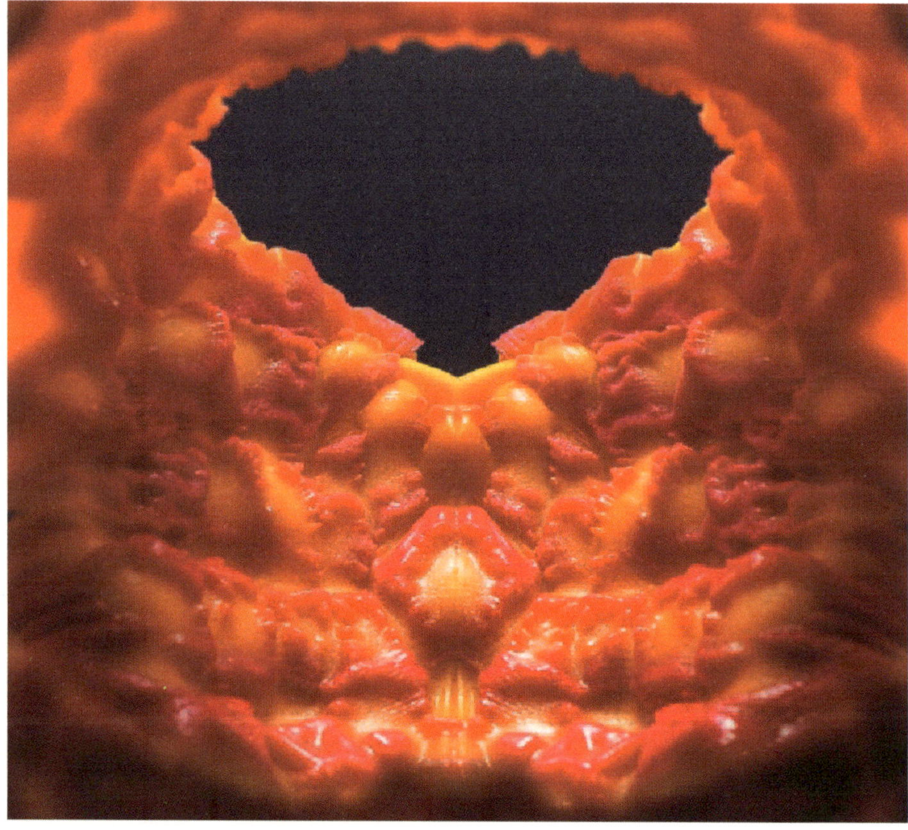

Acknowledgements

This work was supported in part by an NSF EAGER grant award 1152550 "Bio-Beams: Functionally Graded Rapid Design & Fabrication". The work was also supported in part by the Institute for Collaborative Biotechnologies through grant W911NF-09-0001 from the U.S. Army Research Office. The content of the information does not necessarily reflect the position or the policy of the Government, and no official endorsement should be inferred.

The *Imaginary Beings* collection was fabricated and sponsored by Objet Ltd. (Multi- Material 3D Printing) and created in close collaboration with W. Craig Carter (Department of Materials Science and Engineering, MIT) and Joe Hicklin (The Mathworks). Other contributors include Dr. James Weaver (Wyss Institute, Harvard University), Turlif Vilbrandt (Symvol, Uformia), Kevin Cohan (The Mathworks), Sarah Zaranek (The Mathworks), and Seth DeLand (The Mathworks). The author also wishes to thank our network of colleagues and advisors of MIT including Prof. Christine Ortiz, Prof. Mary C. Boyce, Prof. Lorna Gibson and Prof. David Wallace.

References:

Fryazinov O., Fayolle P. A., et al. "Feature-based volumes for implicit intersections". In *Computers & Graphics*, 2011.

Jencks, Charles. *The Language of Post-modern Architecture.* Rizzoli Intl, 1984.

Kahn, Louis. *Conversations With Students.* Princeton Architectural Press, 1969.

Oxman, Neri. *Material-based Design Computation* (Ph.D. thesis). MIT, 2010.

Oxman, Neri. "Variable Property Rapid Prototyping". In *Journal of Virtual and Physical Prototyping (VPP)*, vol.6, nr.1 (2011A), pp. 3-31.

Oxman, Neri. "Finite Element Synthesis. Proceedings of VRAP: Advanced Research in Virtual and Rapid Prototyping". In Bártolo Paulo Jorge et al. *Innovative Developments in Virtual and Physical Prototyping.* Taylor & Francis, 2011B.

Oxman N., Keating S. and Tsai E. "Functionally Graded Rapid Prototyping. Proceedings of VRAP: Advanced Research in Virtual and Rapid Prototyping". In Bártolo Paulo Jorge et al. *Innovative Developments in Virtual and Physical Prototyping.* Taylor & Francis, 2011C.

Oxman, Neri. "Programming Matter. Architectural Design, Special Issue: Material Computation: Higher Integration". In *Morphogenetic Design*, Vol.82, Issue 2 (March/April 2012), pp. 88-95. Guest edited by Achim Menges.

Semper, Gottfried. *The Four Elements of Architecture and Other Writings (RES monographs in anthropology and aesthetics).* Cambridge: Cambridge University Press; New York, 1851.

Sennett, Richard. *The Craftsman.* Yale University Press, 2008.

Thom, René. "Introduction, Form and Structural Stability". In *Structural Stability and Morphogenesis; an Outline of a General Theory of Models.* 1st English ed. by W. A. Benjamin, Reading, Mass (1975).

Thompson, D'Arcy Wentworth. *On Growth and Form.* Cambridge: The University Press, new ed., 1942.

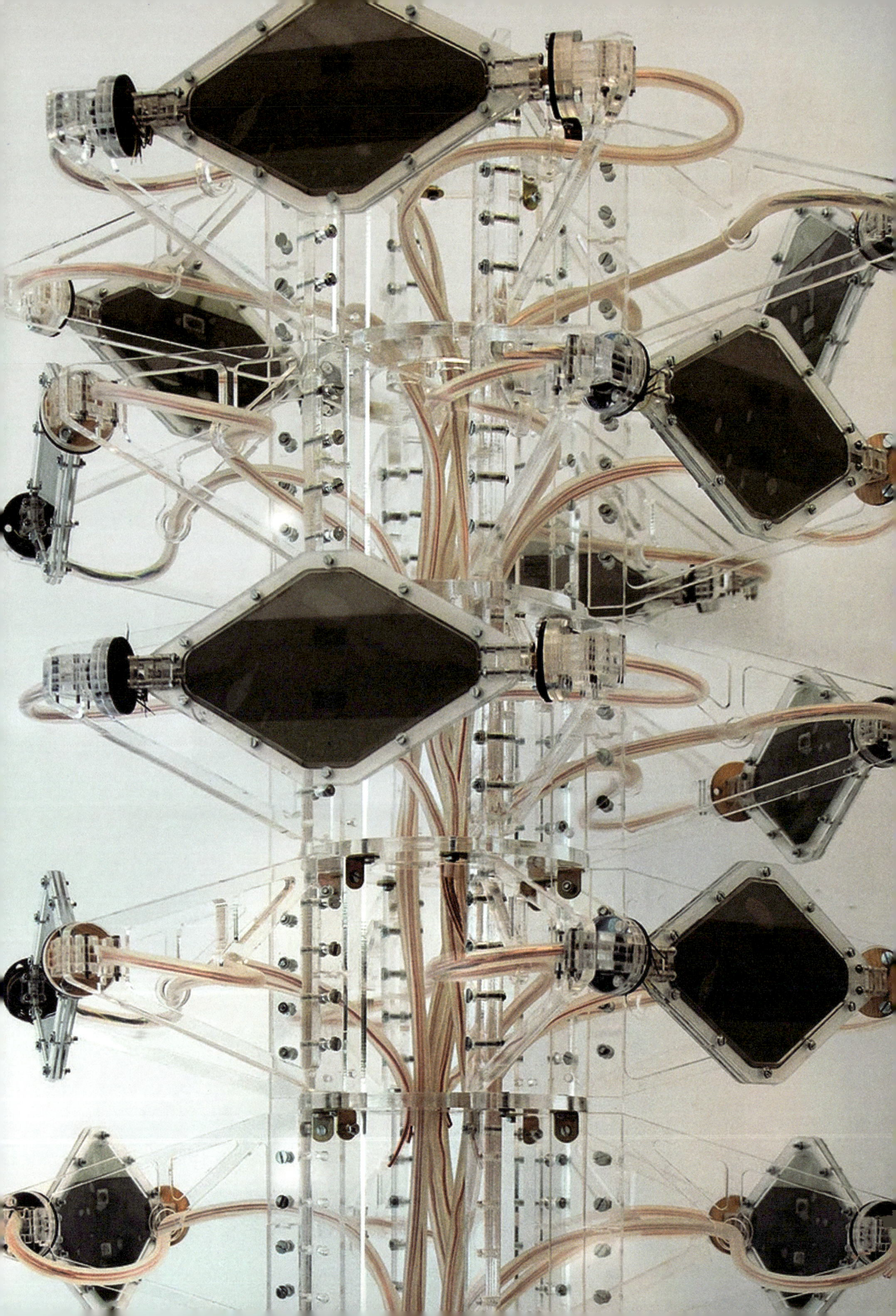

Matterlessness
On Architecture, Materiality and Form under the Allonomous Condition

Jordi Vivaldi

In experimental academic architecture and over the past decade, the term "matter" has achieved great popularity. Its meaning has definitivelly moved away from the neutral and flat mold posed by Aristotle, acquiring in the last centuries and through the concepts of "truthfulness" and "vitalism" some of the features traditionally ascribed to "form".

The aim of this article is to argue that the current culmination of this process is triggered by the technological circumstance characteristic of the Allonomous Condition and, paradoxically, does not imply the radicalization or re-interpretation of "matter", but its replacement by "form". This reflection is particularly manifested in most of the contemporary projects that revolve around the expression "Black Ecologies". In this article, it is applied to three of its most well known representatives: BitMap Printing, Slow Furl, and BIK house.

The argument developed is twofold: on the one hand, it states the relevance that the notions of "information", "performance" and "platform" have acquired in certain sectors of experimental architecture, and, on the other hand, it affirms the intimate relationship between these three notions and the concept of "form".

Previous page:
BioCatalytic Cell. Project of IaaC, developed at Master in Advanced Architecture 02 in 2016/17. Researchers: Thora H. Arnardottir, Jessica Dias, Christopher Wong; Faculty: Chiara Farinea, Carmelo Zappulla, Paolo Bombelli, Maria Kuptsova; Guest Advisor: Claudia Pasquero; Biology Support: Nuria Conde Pueyo.

Throughout the 20th century, modern architecture has generally interpreted the notion of matter from an Aristotelian point of view. Under this scenario, matter was merely read as opposed to form: "Whereas form must have some kind of shape, matter is that which escapes this shape and resists taking on definite contours".[1] After the Pythagoreans,[2] matter acquired, in opposition to form, an intense negative sense. Consequently, in this context our knowledge of the mathematical structure of objects took precedence over the messy matter from which those objects are made.

Beginning with these postulates, and supported by Platonic physics, whose geometry based on regular polyhedra redeemed the world from its sullied material condition, Aristotle established his hylomorphic model. Under this scenario, the world is divided between form and matter: the latter consists in a homogeneous, passive, formless and receptive element that is in need of a "form", an intangible "pattern" imposed upon it from outside in order to provide structure and identity.

In that sense, the terms "matter" and "pattern" corresponded to the words for "mother" and "father" as they were understood in ancient Greece – in other words, as receiving and giving entities, respectively.

One of the most obvious examples of the application of this ancestral framework to architecture is that of concrete. It behaves like an authentic "matter" – i.e., a passive, neutral and homogeneous mass capable of acquiring the most fanciful of forms through a formwork system. Its habitual white color demonstrates the desire to exalt the intelligible purity of forms. Le Corbusier was precisely referring to this when he affirmed that "whitewash is absolute; on it, everything stands out, inscribes itself absolutely; it is sincere and loyal".[3] According to this framework, and through geometry and proportion, the architect is constituted as a demiurge, that is, as a being capable of acting from a transcendent plane and endowing, as if by miracle, a structuring form to plain matter.

Construction detail, Auguste Choisy, 1873

Goetheanum, Rudolf Steiner, 1928

Concrete has been the quintessential 20th-century material. From the first buildings by Perret (Rue Franklin, 1904) to the latest structures by architects like Jean Nouvel (Agbar, 2005), authors working from diverse ideologies – from Le Corbusier to Eisenman, Wright and Rossi – have all used concrete as a fundamental material in their designs. However, since the 19th century certain minoritarian currents in architecture have made an effort to legitimate "matter" through an incremental process of formalization.

This article argues that this process culminates in the 21st century with the concepts of "information", "performance" and "platform" generalized by the age of Antrobology,[4] an expression coined by Eric Sadin in order to underline the radical intertwining between bodies and algorithms defined by our current technologies.
This technological circumstance occurs under a very specific contemporaneous condition defined in this paper as "Alllonomous".[5] This notion builds on the kantian concepts of heteronomy and autonomy. It essentially consists in the recognizement of the capacity of all objects to produce it's own "nomos", that is to say, it's own "form", independently of their human, ecologic, zoologic or algorithmic nature. During the XX, matter has gradually replaced its attributes with those of form, absorbing its qualities of structure, pro-activity and heterogeneity. However, before the XX century architecture has embodied this recovery process through two concepts that have been fundamental in order to trigger this long-term task: truthfulness and vitalism.[6]

Matter's recovery in architecture: From truthfulness to vitalism

The concept of truthfulness in architecture should be read in opposition to the idealism of authors like Alberti or Palladio. In his Re-aedificatoria, Alberti claimed that "architecture is not about artisan techniques but about "cose mentale"".[7] What concerned him were not material attributes such as color or texture, but the geometrical proportions of the forms that he produced with matter. This statement becomes very evident in his façade for the Palazzo Rucellai (Alberti, 1446). Conversely, some centuries later authors like Ruskin, Viollet-le-Duc or Semper defended the relevance of matter in architecture, asserting that the choice of a material should depend on the laws dictated by its nature, such that "brick should look like brick; wood, wood; iron, iron, each according to its own mechanical laws".[8] Rondelet and Choissy also gave importance to the truth of the material, particularly throughout their exhaustive constructive drawings. However, this group of authors still remained idealistic. The use of materials always had unbreachable limits, determined by the idea that the architectural object was intended to express. In that sense, and although its internal structure was recognized, matter was still subordinate to an external idea, that is to say, to an external form.

Einstein Tower, Erich Mendelsohn, 1921

Truthfulness was just a first step in this process of redemption, however. Some decades later, in his Vie des Formes (1881) Henri Focillon alluded to the vitalist capacities of matter, emphasizing its capacity of movement and metamorphosis. Already present in the Baroque and empowered by the Enlightenment idea of "natura naturans", concepts like the Bildungstriet, the Thatkraft or the Urpflanze of Goethe articulated a vitalist approach to matter that was very closely related to German Expressionism.

Ruskin and Semper's seminal materialism based on the idea of the truth of materials gave way to a radical pragmatism in which architects had no objection to working with hybridized, heterogeneous or artificial materials, because what was relevant was not the shape of the material, but its analogies with natural metamorphosis. Many glass-based projects from the early 20th century replicate these morphogenetic processes, an attitude that in a certain manner was already present in the gothic. In this sense and in resonance with the “élan vital”[9] of Bergson, certain uses of concrete were quite adequate to this aim: its fluidity permitted to imitate the formal exuberance of some morphogenetic natural processes, as we can see in the Goetheanum (Steiner, 1928) or the Einstein Tower (Mendelsohn, 1921). Moreover, this relation was not only metaphorical but also performative: the use of concrete allowed for establishing a certain continuity between form and structure, something that was characteristic of the organic beings that were so greatly admired at that time. As a consequence, a progressive material vitalism was thus constituted, which, however, also had its conservative reverse. Fueled by the phenomenological work of Rasmussen and Norberg-Schulz, architects as Herzog & Meuron, Steven Holl or Peter Zumthor propose a haptic approach to architecture that relies on materials as symbolic shapers of architectural space. Under this scenario and in close relation to Merleau-Ponty’s notion of “flesh”,[10] matter is understood as the repository of a tactile and cultural memory that stands in contrast to the supposed technical and ideological alienation of modernity.

In parallel to the general disdain that Modernism showed for materiality during the first half of the 20th century, truthfulness and vitalism have gradually contributed to the reconsideration of matter as a substance with a certain agency.
This process was based not on the exaltation of the passivity, neutrality and homogeneity that originally characterized matter, but through the importation of attributes from the notion of form.

The truthfulness argued by Ruskin is based precisely on the understanding that matter has a specific inner “character” that makes it heterogeneous, while the vitalism of Steiner alludes to the metamorphic capacities of living beings.

However, both cases remain idealistic. Truthfulness asserts the need for an external form to choose the matter that best suits to its purposes. Vitalism claims that matter should be seen as a material of organic expression that still needs an artist or architect to unveil its aesthetic potentialities of metamorphosis.

In both cases, matter is still seen not just in opposition to form but also under its control: the vitalism defended by Bergson differs from the vitalism of Deleuze in the sense that, for the former, matter is still a generic substance that needs an artist to particularize it.

Conversely, for Deleuze, matter is an immanent reality: it provides form to itself and does not require any transcendental agent.

Information, Performance and Platforms under the Allonomous Condition

Over the last decade, a new ontological, social and technological approach has fueled the emergence of Allonomy,[11] a condition that builds on the kantian notions of heteronomy and autonomy. In close relation to XXI century ontological, sociological and technological approaches, the Allonomous Condition consists in the recognizement of the capacity of all objects to produce it's own "nomos", that is to say, it's own "form", independently of their human, ecologic, zoologic or algorithmic nature. Our technological present has not been impermeable to this condition, and advances such as artificial intelligence or machine learning are precise articulations of it. Faced with of a dual ontology that is no longer alluding to Heideggerian human nudity but to a planet inhabited by algorithmic beings that live with and against us, Eric Sadin defines our technological circumstance as antrobological.

This notion expresses the "increasingly dense intertwining between organic bodies and "immaterial elfs" (digital codes) that sketches a complex and singular composition which is determined to evolve continually, contributing to the instauration of a condition which is inextricably mixed -human/artificial-".[12]

Indeed, the propagation of artificial intelligence and the multi-scalar robotization of the organic establishes, in addition to a change of medium, a change of condition: its algorithmic power does not merely offer itself as an automatic pilot for daily life, but it also triggers a radical transformation of our human nature, setting up a perennial and universal intertwining in between bodies and information. In this sense, the multidisciplinar generalisation of machine learning, the progress in genetic engineering or the robotization of the mundane no longer refer to a humanity that is merely improved or enriched, but to a humanity that is intertwined: it is unfolded through a physiological platform that is woven by algorithmic, organic robotic and ecologic agents whose symbiosis is not metaphorical or narrative, but strictly performative. Antrobology points to an age that is characterized by the intimate and profound hybridization of the human being with its "others": they are no longer constituted as environments or external devices that are occasionally available to the human being, but as informational inner dimensions whose performance is no longer completely under human control. It is precisely under this scenario that "artificial extelligence" becomes "artificial intelligence": through an exercise of "in-corporation" that is fundamental, the intelligence, the eidos, what has traditionally been understood as form, is no longer an external entity that articulates matter from outside. Instead, it replaces matter by operating as an integrative, digital, interior and molecular structure that performs at every level of scale and that prevents us from understanding where exactly we can identify this raw, passive and formless matter.

This plural understanding of the subject established by the Allonomous Condition has not only transformed our approach to human and non-human beings; it also suggests a renewed understanding of the concept of nature in which the idea of "original matter" is also problematic. In that sense, nature is no longer associated with the Green Ecology characteristic of the turn of the century; rather, it emerges as part of a conglomerate that has been defined with the expression "Black Ecologies". This new ecological understanding is no longer the response to a natural crisis. It is not meant to offer salvation from an apocalyptic dystopia or to redeem the excesses of modern man. Neither does it offer the nostalgic protection of a virgin nature: it does not yearn for a green planet or exalt sustainability as a technocratic elixir. The notion of Black Ecologies is the accelerated reaction to an ontological crisis: that of naturalism, of positivism, of relativism. It stages resistance to a hierarchical understanding of the world that still operates based on a 1000-year-old dichotomy: the confrontation between nature and artifice as irreconcilable opposites.

In the wake of thinkers like Timothy Morton, Slavoj Žižek or Bruno Latour, the idea of Black Ecologies not only challenges the boundaries between life and non-life, organic and inorganic, human and inhuman but offers, above all, a revised narrative. Leaving behind the contemplative, harmonic, cyclical and normative Mother Nature that Semper, Ruskin and Viollet le Duc were idealizing in order to emphasize matter through its truthfulness, a techno-natural continuum emerges in its place: operative, chaotic, unpredictable and manipulable, it performs as artifice rather than artifact. It does not function solely as a hyper-technological gadget but constructs a collective fiction: it renounces a secularized garden of Eden to speculate instead about a subject that has become "a nomad assembly in a shared life space that it does not control or own. S/he just occupies it, always in community with biological, technological and cultural others".[13] In this scenario, Green Ecology is revealed as a new opium for the masses: a reactionary force that imposes an unquestionable authority, obstructs alternatives, identifies sins, applies punishments and, above all, defines moral values. In return, it offers a "promised land": the return to an immaculate nature, purified through the domestication of a modern man whose excessive artificiality has transformed the planet into a denatured place.

The logic of Black Ecologies is just the opposite. Faced with a hyper-technified world, more technology. Faced with an inhuman world, more otherness. Faced with an alienated world, more emancipation. And, above all, faced with an adulterated world, more artifice. Biological agents, ecological agents, technological agents and cultural agents cooperate in a reality that is no longer constructed based on Promethean epics, relativist ironies or primitivist nostalgia, but accelerated hybrids: i.e., poly-plural constructs hurtling toward a post-capitalist world.

In the light of this narrative, Black Ecologies deploys architectural matter based not only on specificity, hyper-realism and processes, but above all based on heterogeneities, structures and pro-activity. it no longer takes shelter in abstraction, historicity or language, but is constituted as an informational and performative platform: operative, corrupt, rugged, disturbed and definitely dark. Under this scenario, the mysterious and the strange do not legitimate contemporary architectural matter through the original truthfulness of Ruskin or the metaphoric vitalism of Steiner, but through an informational performance that is more disturbing than it is salvific: it confirms that there is no longer an outside, that there can no longer be life stripped bare, that there is no longer a pure and transcendent nature to which we can always return. The promiscuous matter of Black Ecologies is revealed as an accelerated and accelerative substance in an increasingly artificialized society, which assumes that the future is a better guide for the present than the past.[14]

The historical and incremental process of matter legitimation, based initially on the truthfulness of Ruskin and the vitalism of Steiner, culminates today with the celebration of the notions of platform, information and performance that singularize Antrobology as defined by Sadin. It is crucial to note here not only that all three terms include the particle "form", but that actually relate to the three main attributes of form: structure (information), activity (performance) and matryoshka (platform). While matter "is that which resist taking any definite contour",[15] form refers to the active presence of a distinguished and qualified structure that contain other forms and that can occasionally change and establish relationships. In opposition to shape, form "is not a mere visual look: its presence operates at every level of scale".[16] It is under this framework that we should read the terms "platform", "information" and "performance".

BitMap Printing, Neri Oxman, 2014.

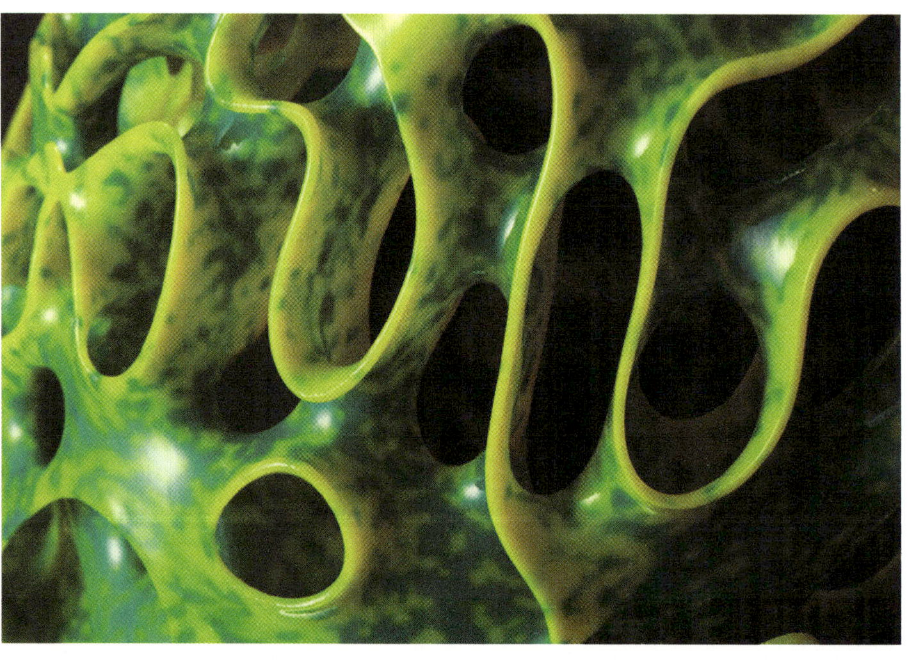

To provide a "platform" means to provide the conditions for an evolving "intertwining" in between forms that is not arbitrary, but that pursues a particular purpose. However, these conditions are never flat and neutral, but are formed, establishing a matryoshka structure of forms inside other forms. To "inform" someone or something means to "structure" that someone or something. It consists precisely in dissolving its neutrality in order to establish an order both in time and space. However, given that every entity has already a form and we cannot imagine a formless element, to inform means actually to transform.

To "perform", in contrast, means to be radically present: it produces an operative impact on the set of conditions in which it is placed, instead of merely symbolizing a non-present entity. The radicality of this presence is currently central in Queer aesthetics through Butler's analysis of "performative expressions",[17] and it contrasts with the distant referent alluded by the symbol or the metaphor. Under this technological condition and through these three elements, the disorder, passivity and homogeneity that traditionally identified matter are replaced by those characteristics that originally qualified form: structure (information), activity (performance) and matryoshka (platform).

However, if the process of legitimation of matter is rooted in replacing its attributes for those of form, it is increasingly more unsustainable to keep referring to it as "matter", when actually, and especially in Antrobology, matter is empty of matter and full of form.

Indeed, under this scenario, experimental architecture proposes a renewed notion of matter whose legitimation, as we will see through some real projects in the following lines, is founded on the three elements that we just mentioned: First, matter is now understood as a platform: it provides not just the conditions of possibility for intertwinings, but it permits as well the presence of forms inside other forms. Second, matter is now informed: it contains a digital or a physical structure that operates at every level of scale. Third, matter now performs: it has an operative presence that is not merely metaphorical or symbolic.

In the field of experimental architectural matter, this approach suggests a new reading of its projects, which paradoxically, is a formal interpretation rather than a materialistic one. However, it is not "formal" in the common understanding articulated by Eisenman or Rossi. It does not assert that there is no excess beneath the architectural forms that are given, rather, as Graham Harman puts it very nicely, it affirms that "the excess is itself always formed".[18] Three projects of experimental architectural matter will help us to solidify these reflections.

From matter to form in experimental architecture materiality

BitMap Printing, Slow Furl, and BIK House are conventionally seen as architecture whose main contribution lies in the renovation of the notion of matter, usually refered to as behavioral matter, living matter, ecological matter, digital matter, expanded matter, data-driven matter or intelligent matter.

However, the relevance of this matter's renovation does not lie in the exaltation or in the re-interpretation of the characteristics that are usually associated to this term, but in its replacement by formal attributes rooted in the categories of information, performance and platform that qualify matter in all those expressions. In the first case, the project Bitmap Printing by Nery Oxman is a set of spongy 3D-printed material into which synthetically processed microorganisms are infiltrated. Through their biological processes they are able to provide oxygen, light, nutrients and energy to the users in hostile environments, such as other planets. The project is located at the intersection between multi-material 3D-printing and synthetic biology, under an entirely operative and manipulable understanding of nature and with the objective of generating self-sufficient human micro-habitats.

The proposal is classified by its author as "Material Ecology". Oxman defines this expression as "an emerging field in design denoting informed relations between products, buildings, systems and their environment".[19] The architect uses the term "informed", referring to information and therefore alluding to the inner structure of the matter that she is fabricating, a peculiarity that confirms the relevance of the Age of Antrobology in experimental architecture. However, if "matter" is informed, it is no longer a homogeneous and amorphous matter, but it contains a digital or a physical structure that operates at every level of scale. Each one of the pieces acts as a platform that hosts intertwinings between natural, human and algorithmic agents. Their activity has performative consequences, because they do not symbolize non-present entities, rather they operate on the set of conditions in which they are inscribed. In this sense, given that each of the pieces is informed, acts as a platform and performs, it is hardly understandable why we refer to them as a specific configuration of matter rather than as a particular type of form.

In recent years, Mette Thomsen from CITA has also investigated new materialities. Notable among the series of projects is Slow Furl (2012), a textile installation that engages with and reacts to human occupation: the "expanded fabric" retreats and contorts slowly as the user moves, continuously generating surprising spatial shapes. However, it is not in this sense that the project accepts a formal reading, but in the embedding of structure, pro-activity and heterogeneity in the fabric: as opposed to acting as a passive receptacle, as would be the case with a conventional fabric, Slow Furl generates a true performative artefact that operates with its own patterns of action and reaction, without receiving any "form" from outside. The textile is digitally informed with a system of sensors that activate a series of micro-controllers, which manifests the deep intertwining of bodies and data that characterizes the Age of Antrobology. The combination of its own activation processes and the shared intertwining mechanisms lets us understand the artefact as a textile platform: when a user touches the fabric and senses the pulse that supports it, its sensory-mechanical system folds and twists into a series of different configurations that never repeat or accumulate, letting users sit, lean or lie down depending on the configuration. Therefore, the project has form at every scale of time and space. Its presence is not evident only in its external contours, but also at the molecular level, since it is structured through flows of information that allow the artefact to perform in time. Similar projects, like those developed by Areti Markopoulou or Carlo Ratti would be aligned with these reflections.

On a bigger scale, the BIK House (2016) in Hannover, is probably one of the most popular built examples of a façade made out of what has been defined as "living matter". It consists of a series of micro-algae panels whose performance produces energy. In this case, and in contrast to the great Media-TIC building by Enric Ruiz Geli, the virtues of the façade are based on the notion of form and not of shape: whereas the façade of the Media-TIC building draws mainly on a geometric operativity based on the overlapping of positive and negative patterns to let the sun in or protect against it, the building by BIK harnesses a chemical performance that breathes and digests. This project proposes a formal reading because its singularity lies in a heterogeneous pro-active structure, although its scale is molecular and its performance independent from the general contour of the architectural object.

Slow Furl, Mette Ramsgard Thomsen, 2008.

Biq House, Arup, 2013.

As in the previous cases, the BIK House façade does not have any of the attributes that traditionally characterize matter: what is relevant from the expression "living matter" is not the term "matter" but the term "living". Being "alive" implies a condition which, above all, is formal: it lies in what Maturana and Varela define as an individual organization that "self-constructs through the recursive production of components".[20] The algae façade system has a molecular structure that performs with a very particular purpose, and therefore remains far removed from the passivity and homogeneity that characterizes the notion of "matter". Most of the projects by architects such as Poletto-Pasquero, P. Beesley or M. Cruz could be read in a similar manner.

Conclusion

Although these three projects are commonly known by their renovated approach to "matter", what is relevant in order to understand their contemporary relevance is not their attachment to the characteristics of matter, but to those of form. As we have seen, Sadin's Antrobology culminates matter's recovery process, which began with the truthfulness of Ruskin and the vitalism of Steiner. However, paradoxically, this culmination means at the same time the obsolescence of the term in experimental architecture.

As Graham Harman mentions, although what is admirable in materialism is its sense that any visible situation contains a deeper surplus able to subvert or surprise it,[21] the kind of formalism approached here does not deny this surplus, it merely states that this surplus is also formed.

But what is crucial is not just the fact that these projects contain form, but also and especially the fact that it is precisely this form that identifies them. Indeed, specific formal arrangements are what is referred to in the first term of expressions such as "intelligent matter, ecological matter, data-driven matter, systemic matter, etc". All of them refer to particular spatio-temporal structures, articulations, organizations, distributions, performances, platforms, informations, operations etc. which, through a digital or/and physical medium, express a particular form that support the project.

Under this scenario, and specifically in the case of "Black Ecologies", in what sense should we keep using the term "matter"? How is it relevant? And more specifically, which of its attributes is still active in these projects? The process of "in-corporation" performed in Antrobology through the replacement of artificial extelligence by artificial intelligence illustrates from a technological perspective the need for moving past the binomial "matter vs form". Instead, rather than approaching experimental architectural materials as living, intelligent, digital or ecological singularities that emerge from a continuous undefined and non-existent raw matter, they should be read as forms, that is to say, as different informational platforms of spatiotemporal structures that perform at every level of scale.

References :

1. Harman, Graham. "Materialism Is Not the Solution". In *The Nordic Journal of Aesthetics*, nr. 47 (2014), p. 100.

2. The experiments with musical strings led by the Pythagoreans to conclude that their sonority did not depend on the material from which their lyres were made, but rather on the geometric series that determine musical intervals.

3. The quote comes from the review of the Salon d'Automne of 1922, published by Jeanneret in *L' Esprit Nouveau.*

4. Sadin, Eric. *La humanidad aumentada*. Buenos Aires: La Caja Negra (2013), pp. 149-155.

5. Vivaldi, Jordi. The Allonomous Condition (Lecture at the University of Trento on 04/04/2019).

6. Prieto, Eduardo. *La vida de la materia*. Madrid: Ediciones Asimétricas (2018), pp. 28-102.

7. Alberti, Leon Battista. *Re-Aedificatoria*. Madrid: Ediciones Asimétricas (2012), p. 21.

8. Semper, Gottfried. *The Four Elements of Architecture and Other Writings*. Cambridge University Press (1969), pp. 45-73.

9. The concept of Élan Vital was introduced by Henri Bergson in his seminal work "Creative Evolution". It is a hypothetical force that explains the evolution and development of organisms.

10. The notion of "flesh" combines physical materiality with all kinds of impulses, desires, appetites, fears, etc. Under this concept, object and subject are constituted with the same materiality.

11. Vivaldi, Jordi. The Allonomous Condition (Lecture at the University of Trento on 04/04/2019).

12. Sadin, Eric. *La humanidad aumentada*. Buenos Aires: La Caja Negra (2013), p.152.

13. Braidotti, Rosi. *Lo posthumano*. Barcelona: Geidsa Editorial (2015), p. 229.

14. Avanessian A. and Reis M. "Introducción". In *Aceleracionismo*. Buenos Aires: Ed. Caja Negra (2017), p. 25.

15. Harman, Graham. "Materialism is Not the Solution". In *The Nordic Journal of Aesthetics*, nr. 47 (2014), p. 100.

16. Harman, Graham. "Materialism is Not the Solution". In *The Nordic Journal of Aesthetics*, nr. 47 (2014), p. 102.

17. Butler, Judith. *Notes towards a performative theory of assamblage*. Cambridge: Harvard University Press (2015).

18. Harman, Graham. "Materialism is Not the Solution". In *The Nordic Journal of Aesthetics*, nr. 47 (2014), p. 100.

19. Oxman, Neri. "Material Ecology". In *Proceedings of the 32nd Annual Conference of the Association for Computer Aided Design in Architecture* ACADIA (2012), pp. 19-20.

20. Maturana H. and Varela F. "Describing the logic of the living. The adequacy and limitations of the idea of autopoiesis. In Zeleny, M. (ed.). "Autopoiesis, Dissipative Structures and Spontaneous Social Orders". AAAS Selected Symposium 55. Boulder: Westview Press (1980), p. 23.

21. Harman, Graham. "Materialism is Not the Solution". In *The Nordic Journal of Aesthetics*, nr. 47 (2014), p. 100.

WWW.IAAC.NET
WWW.IAACBLOG.COM

Previous page figure:
Algaetecture. Project of IaaC, developed at Master in Advanced Architecture 01 in 2015/16. Researchers: Andre Resende Mohamad Atab Hsin Li Stefan Fotev Sureshkumar Kumaravel Yasamin Khalilbeigi; Faculty: Claudia Pasquero, Carmelo Zappulla, Maria Kupstova.

IAAC BITS n. 9
BLACK ECOLOGIES
Advanced Architecture Magazine

Edited by
Manuel Gausa, Areti Markopoulou, Jordi Vivaldi

With contributions by
M.Gausa, A.Markopoulou, F.Roche, V.Guallart, C.Pasquero, M.Poletto, R.Rubio, R.Iancu, K.Larina, T.Gorbachewskaya, M.Joachim, Noumena, M.Cruz, A.Adamatzky, E.Kac, N.Oxman, J. Vivaldi

IAAC BITS MAGAZINE

Published by
Institute for Advanced Architecture of Catalonia , Barcelona
www.iaac.net

Indexing
ISSN 2339-8647
ISBN: English 978-84-120885-0-2
Printed in Comgrafic, Barcelona

Publication date
September 2019

Distribution
Actar D, Inc. New York, Barcelona.
New York
440 Park Avenue South, 17th Floor
New York, NY 10016, USA
T +1 2129662207
salesnewyork@actar-d.com

Barcelona
Roca i Batlle 2-4
08023 Barcelona, Spain
T +34 933 282 183
eurosales@actar-d.com

Contact communications & publications office:
info@iaac.net
chiara.cesareo@iaac.net

https://iaac.net/iaac-bits-about/